Knit to Fit

*A comprehensive guide
to hand and machine
knitting and crochet*

SECOND EDITION

Knit to Fit

IDA RILEY DUNCAN

LIVERIGHT / NEW YORK

2.987654321

Standard Book Number: 47140-520-2
Library of Congress Catalog Card Number: 75-131267
Designed by Madelaine Caldiero
Illustrations by Nancy Lou Gahan

MANUFACTURED IN THE UNITED STATES OF AMERICA

To my late husband, John Brown Duncan

To my daughter, Jean, and to my
daughter, Peggy, whom I wish to thank
for her assistance with the numerous
diagrams without which the book
would have little meaning

To my grandchildren, Shelley, Jock, Dennis,
Lynn, Peter, and Jeffrey

Contents

Knit to Fit

Too many knitters rely upon stereotyped directions, with the result that the work is often too big or too small and generally unsatisfactory. In the first place, one may wish to use different yarn and needles, so that the knitting may be tighter or looser than called for. And few of us are a perfect size 12 or 14. Furthermore, not enough consideration is given to the style that will bring out the best in the wearer. True, an illustration which appears in a knitting manual may be exactly the garment that one wishes, with the exception of the sleeve, or a neckline that may emphasize too broad a chin. How simple it can be to change these details, with no guesswork at all!

Just as in the construction of a beautiful piece of architecture, there are principles which may be followed for correct shaping. No graph paper is necessary. Simple diagrams are all that are needed. It is important to read the principles outlined in "Measurements and Stitch Gauge" (Chap. 3). Once this process is understood, there will be no cupping of skirts or too-tight garments

1
Scientific Approach to Knitting

across the bust; and you will realize that with correct styling, anyone can look stylish in a knit.

It should be stressed here that this is the author's scientific, exclusive formula method.

No matter what your objective in studying the course, the following four "musts" will aid in your development, either for yourself, in teaching others, or as a designer.

- ► Become style conscious
- ► Become figure conscious
- ► Become color conscious
- ► Become personality conscious

From now on, look through magazines and newspapers with a critical eye. Clothes consciousness is easy to acquire this way. Keep for reference or for file anything that particularly interests you. This collecting does not refer to knit styles alone but to any style that is adaptable for knit or crochet.

DESIGNING KNITS

If you wish to design or be an instructor of knits, whether for hand or machine, you must learn to diagram and chart directions. You cannot understand or teach others by literally reading a printed page. You yourself must be able to plan a knitted garment, stitch by stitch. There are no stereotyped directions for creative fashion, including design of garments. Each special problem in shaping is discussed individually as it is reached in a lesson.

This is a new method, a simple-formula method that will enable you to chart any style or size of garment, using any suitable material, with the assurance that it is going to fit perfectly without any cutting or stretching. And you must realize that any type of garment can be knitted. The only limitations are good taste and the basic rules of design. As stated, there are four "musts" that will aid in your development. Follow these and do not miss an opportunity!.

American women generally are becoming accustomed to the type and color of clothes which are most becoming, regardless of the dictates of fashion. After you have studied this course, you will be able to diagram and chart clothes that are chic, bring out the good points while concealing the poor, and choose a becoming color. One must remember that style and color have a great effect upon morale. Women should keep their charm and femininity at all times.

Chapter 34 includes a section on color, which will aid you in becoming color-conscious. Read this part carefully now at the beginning of the course.

If you own a yarn shop or instruct others, gradually draw diagrams for your customers. Hours of time are saved, not writing but diagramming. Of course, you will not say exactly how you arrived at the figures. And, if you wish to use styles from the knitting manuals, you will be able to change directions to suit individual needs. You will be surprised at the prestige you will gain. Satisfied customers bring other customers.

Later, we shall discuss machine-made garments and the reasons for their sameness. We shall also suggest means to correct this monotony of style. Like anything original and custom-made, individual hand-knits should have a beauty all their own.

MATERIALS

The study of yarns is very difficult in the United States. In Canada, the British Isles, etc., one knows the thickness of the yarn by the number of folds or plys. Not so in America. Another confusing thing is that manufacturers and distributors have different names for similar yarns. I suggest you spend some time studying materials in the better shops. Do not become confused. It takes time to know knitting materials.

The following are some of the more general yarns:

Knitting worsted.   Knitting worsted is a hard-wearing, 4-ply yarn—a good yarn with which to start a beginner. It is suitable for heavier sweaters, mittens, gloves, caps, etc.

For knitting, the needles that are the easiest to handle are American Standard #5 to #7 (English Standard #8 to #6) aluminum, short.

For crochet, #00 Steel Needle Double Knitting Worsted, American Standard #10, or English Standard #3 needles are excellent for skating- or ski-sweaters.

If one uses too large needles, the garment stretches abominably, both for knit and crochet; and if knitted tightly, one should never have more than 6 stitches to the inch for Knitting Worsted.

Germantown.   Germantown is a soft, 4-ply yarn, light in weight. It is good for baby blankets, afghans, robes, etc., but too soft for general wear. Use the same needles as for Knitting Worsted, either for knitting or crochet.

Sport yarn.   Sport Yarn is still a worsted yarn and 4-ply but finer than Knitting Worsted, so the finished product is not as heavy. It is suitable for sportswear of all kinds: shifts, classic blouses, mini dresses, etc. For knitting, the best needles are American Standard #3 to #5 (English Standard #10 to #8).

For crochet, I consider Sports Yarn much more attractive than Knitting Worsted for long sleeveless sweaters, crocheted "shells," mini dresses. Use a #5 steel needle. To me, however, loosely crocheted, sleeveless sweaters, long weskits, etc. will always appear ugly and "sloppy," and may tend to lose their shape when washed. For any such garment, I suggest you use lightweight yarn, of which there are many, and smaller needles.

Saxony. Saxony, often called Baby Yarn, may be bought in 2-, 3-, or 4-ply. It is extremely soft and suitable for all baby things.

There are countless other yarns, some springy, of all wool, mohair, rayon, wool and nylon, silk, acrilan, straw, and many novelty yarns of silky softness, cool enough for summer wear. Ribbon alone, or ribbon with combinations of yarn or metallic, is very fashionable. It is surprising how ribbons stand wear and look chic for all occasions.

Metallic stripes, beads, sequins, appliqués and embroidery on blouses, sweaters, and evening gowns are tremendously popular.

Exceptions for machine-knitting

There are certain yarns which are difficult or require more care on a machine. On closely-needled machines, for example, in order to knit heavier yarn (e.g. Knitting Worsted), every other needle has to be used. Nubby yarns are apt to catch if the needle is too tight; and if the yarn is composed of two materials, one springy and the other with no elasticity, the yarn often slips off the needles. Angora yarn must be handled with care because it is so soft, breaks easily, and appears flat. Try steaming and shaking.

▸ PROJECT ◂

▶ *Start your files now both on color and garments. (Project refers to the work that is to be done in the lesson. When a diagram and chart are asked for, do not look at the answers at the back of the book, where they are explained in detail. Carefully do as the lessons request, then check your answers.)*

Yarn gauge

The following table suggests the approximate amount of the more common yarns.

SIZE	12	14	16
KNITTING WORSTED			
Coat (long)	36 oz.	38 oz.	40 oz.
Dress	32 oz.	34 oz.	36 oz.
Cardigan	20 oz.	22 oz.	24 oz.
SPORT YARN			
Dress	18 oz.	19 oz.	20 oz.
Cardigan	9 oz.	10 oz.	11 oz.
SHETLAND			
Dress	20 oz.	21 oz.	22 oz.

Sizes of needles and crochet hooks

Needles. Being educated in England, having learned to knit at 5, and having taught there for 6 years, I realize that both English and Canadian knitters, as well as those in other countries, might have difficulties with comparable American needle sizes. The following are the English and Canadian needle sizes compared to the American—bearing in mind that the larger the size, the smaller the needle in English sizes. The English #10 is equivalent to the American #3—consider up and down from there.

ENGLISH, CANADIAN		AMERICAN	
#12	is	#1	
#11	is	#2	
#10	is	#3	
# 9	is	#4	
# 8	is	#5	
# 7	is	#6	
# 6	is	#7	
# 5	is	#8	etc.

Crochet hooks. Crochet hooks are made of steel, composition, or wood. Naturally, the size and type of the hook must be chosen to suit the material. Generally a steel hook is used for cotton thread, and very often for yarn. I consider a #5 steel hook the best for all general purposes.

Steel crochet hooks range in size from #00, the largest, to #14, the smallest. The composition crochet hooks are numbered according to actual size: #1 is the smallest and #9 the largest.

There are also large wooden crochet hooks on the market for rug-making.

You have learned a little about materials. If in doubt about needles for a certain yarn, consult a knitting manual for that type of yarn. If two different sizes are suggested, it is often advisable to use only one size, the intermediate one. Buying two sets of needles as well as material adds to the initial cost and may even become a deterrent to making a first sweater.

2
Fundamentals

DEFINITIONS

Machine knitted

As the name implies, machine knits are manufactured by a machine. There are, however, different types of machine knits.

For the first type, the material is knitted on a machine, then the pieces are marked from a pattern, sewn before cutting so the pieces do not fray, cut, and sewn together.

For the second type, the pieces are shaped on a machine, using different techniques to adjust the shaping. These are a better kind.

If you inquire about the wearability of cheaper machine knits, you will learn that they are generally unsatisfactory: They sag and grow long. But there is still another very important factor. They are "much of a muchness": the same type of neckline, the same short sleeves, and the same narrow ribbed skirt. Pay special attention to these facts and keep away from the undesirable machine-made look.

It should be understood by those who have knitting machines that when making or designing machine knits, one must consider the design of hand-knits first, where all the shaping may be accomplished according to the rules of good dress design. In this case, the directions have to be adjusted according to the limitations of your machine.

Hand-loomed

Rather an ambiguous cognomen, this designation refers to machine-knitted garments, finished by hand, that possess more originality and style than cheaper machine knits.

Hand-knitted

As the name implies, hand-knitted means that the garment has been knitted entirely by hand. If a hand-knitted garment has been designed and charted correctly, it should fit perfectly without any stretching, shrinking, or cutting. I, myself, can chart any garment, for any figure, from the stitch gauge of an experienced knitter, with the assurance that it will not require a fitting. This is to be your aim.

▶ *PROJECT* ◀

► *To practice hand-knitting, make samples of:*

garter stitch (all knitting).
stockinette stitch (knit 1 row, purl 1 row).
ribbing (K. 1, P. 1, and K. 2, P. 2).
decreasing and increasing.
binding off.

► *Use sport yarn with #3 or #4 needles. 24 stitches will suffice, and the sample should be about 2 inches in width.*

► *Remember that women who knit the Continental way, throwing the thread with the left hand, usually knit more loosely. I suggest, therefore, that you use a needle one size smaller than that indicated.*

► *In crochet, the thread should never be wound tightly around the left index finger but should be relaxed at all times.*

KNITTING MACHINE

As all knitting is based on the stockinette stitch, which is the easiest to make on a machine, the following should be thoroughly understood before trying to proceed with any other stitches, as on p. 117, or with the shaping of any garment. (The garter stitch and the moss stitch are impossible to knit on many machines.)

You will notice that many machines have the purl side of the work facing you. This is because the yarn is pulled through the stitches toward you, causing them to make a purl stitch. The stockinette stitch, however, is formed in the same manner as in hand-knitting, with the knit side at the back.

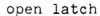

open latch    closed latch

DIAGRAM 1

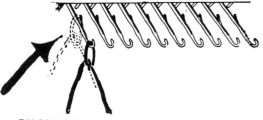

DIAGRAM 2

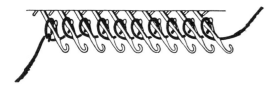

DIAGRAM 3

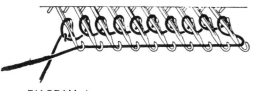

DIAGRAM 4

Make sure to look sideways across the bed of the machine to learn if the latches are open or closed. (Reading glasses are preferable to bifocals when using a machine.)

Casting on

There are two ways to cast on stitches on a machine. For all garments, cast on with closed stitches.

FIRST METHOD

1. Working with the lock or slide at the right, push forward the required number of needles into the working position, making sure there are an equal number on each side of the center.

2. Move the lock backwards and forwards several times to open the latches, leaving the lock or slide on the right-hand side.—Be sure all latches are open. See Diagram 1 for open and closed latches.

3. Fasten the yarn on the last needle at the left, using a slip knot placed behind the open latch. See Diagram 2.

4. Wind the yarn around the individual heads, as in Diagram 3, counter-clockwise, or simply stated, as though writing the small letter "e." Wind the yarn with the right hand and push the previous loop behind the open latch with the left. Note that the yarn must not be drawn too tightly nor placed too far back of the needles.

5. Keep checking to be sure that all latches are open.

6. Lay the yarn the same for the last needle, then *upwards* from right to left on open needles, as in Diagram 4.

Hold the yarn close to the first needle with the right hand, place the yarn across the needles with the left hand, and then let it hang straight down.

7. Move the sliding lock from right to left, working slowly and pressing down lightly for the first row of knit-

ting. Check to see that all latches are open. If not, correct by bringing needle out until the stitch is in back of the latch and the needle is again in working position.

8. Place the yarn from left to right with the open needle heads and move the sliding lock from left to right.

9. Continue knitting in this fashion.

Remember that the yarn and lock or slide should always be in the same direction. The lock moves the needles, thus forcing the stitches to work the latches and form a stitch. Never change the direction of the lock when partly in operation. It must only be worked in one direction.

To remove work from needle, move the lock or slide across the row without laying yarn in position.

SECOND METHOD

This method leaves an open row of stitches at the lower edge. This version is good if one wishes to add to the bottom, for example in ribbing, etc.

1. Place yarn loosely from right to left in the open needle heads.

2. Slide lock to the left, so that the yarn lies in a zigzag position.

3. Place yarn from left to right in needle heads and move sliding lock from left to right forming the first row of knitting.

Increasing

To increase at the edges or at each end, apply to machine knitting the same rules regarding when to increase as those in hand knitting—with the exception that one must know definitely how many rows of machine knitting make ½ inch, 1 inch, etc.

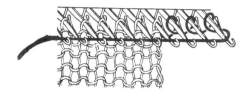

DIAGRAM 5

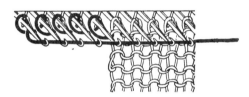

DIAGRAM 6

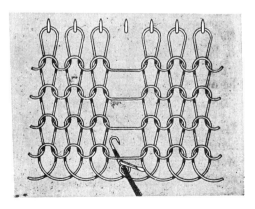

DIAGRAM 7

METHOD

1. Use a finished edge and increase 1 stitch at a time at the edge where the yarn is attached, preferably the right side.

2. Bring the extra needle or needles into working position. Wrap the yarn counter-clockwise around one or more needles as desired. See Diagram 5. Be sure to push the yarn in back of the latch.

3. Work a row.

4. Add a stitch or stitches at the other end, left, wrapping the yarn clockwise, as in Diagram 6.

5. Work a row.

To increase single stitches across a row, it is possible to move a number of stitches outward. See Diagram 7. The stitch below on the adjacent needle of the previous row is placed behind the latch of the empty needle.

Decreasing

To decrease at each end, use the following method. Note that when moving stitches it is important not to twist any. As a guide, keep in mind purling in hand knitting, in which stitches should be picked up from the back, placing one stitch over the other. As in increasing across a row, it is much simpler to change the tension, if appropriate.

METHOD

1. Using a decker, transfer needle or crochet hook, place the last stitch on the next needle and over the second stitch.

2. Be sure to place empty needles out of service, and see that both stitches on the second needle are behind the latch. See Diagram 8.

3. Work a row, then the two stitches are automatically made one. (Note that both ends may be decreased at the same time.)

To decrease across a row, work as follows:

METHOD

1. Where the decrease has to be made, place one stitch over the next stitch, being sure it is behind the latch of the second needle.
2. Move the other stitches into position.
3. Work a row.

Binding off

As in hand knitting, do not pull the yarn too tightly.

METHOD

1. Start binding off at the yarn end, right, one stitch at a time.
2. Place first stitch over second stitch.
3. Put both stitches in back of the latch.
4. Place yarn across the needles in the direction you are working, left. Pull yarn through both stitches. Now there is one stitch instead of two.
5. Place this stitch on the next needle and again pull yarn through. Continue in this manner across the row.

When many stitches have to be bound off, and you want a good-looking edge, I consider it better to knit an extra row, then take the work from the machine. Use an ordinary straight knitting needle, and, taking out one stitch at a time, place the needle in a loop from the back as if to purl. Now bind off the hand way.

Join yarns at the end, if possible. You may, how-

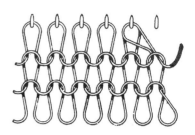

DIAGRAM 8

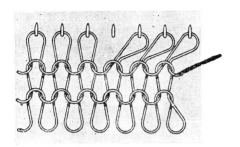

DIAGRAM 9

ever, join in the middle. Place the end yarn from the new ball across the end of attached yarn, in an opposite direction, so there is an overlap of about 4 inches. Both ends of yarn will be worked in.

See the section on ribbing, page 17, and Diagram 9.

▶ **PROJECT** ◀

▸ *Practice all fundamentals before beginning any garment or accessory.*

DIAGRAMMING AND CHARTING

▸ Diagramming is the drawing of each part of the sweater, for example, back, front, and sleeves.

▸ Charting is the putting in of the necessary figures for the shaping of each part.

So that you will understand the basic shaping for an upper garment, we start with the easiest first—a simple sweater. It would be advisable, if time permits, to knit one, as you learn each change of shaping in the following chapters. It may be a slipover or a cardigan (coat-sweater), not shaped at the sides, with any simple neckline (round, turtle, V, or square), and any type of sleeve (long, short, three-quarter, or fitted cap), with or without buttonholes and pockets and, from your stitch gauge and measurements, for either a man, woman, or a child. Whatever you choose, make sure to knit a full-sized garment: I do not advocate knitting small, doll-like garments, because the same principles cannot be followed.

In the process, you will learn to diagram and chart all types of slipovers and cardigans. You can sketch what you desire, or use a picture, or just visualize the style. Absolutely no stereotyped directions are to be used. From the basic shaping of sweaters, you will have good ground-

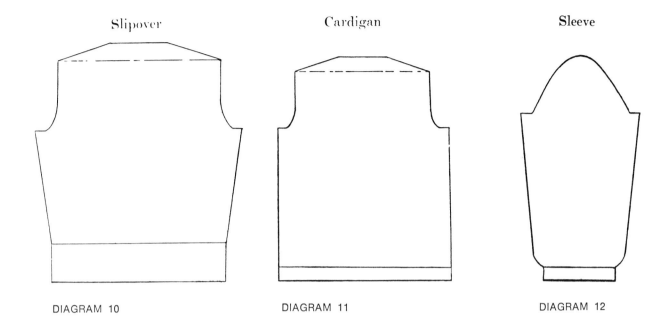

Slipover   Cardigan   Sleeve

DIAGRAM 10   DIAGRAM 11   DIAGRAM 12

work for the shaping of all upper garments. See Diagrams 10, 11, and 12.

Shaping by hand and machine actually go hand-in-hand. In hand-knitting, however, there are both straight and circular needles, whereas circular knitting is found only in very expensive knitting machines. Even there, there are limitations for both circular and straight-needled knitting machines. The main thing is to design the best way possible first, then, if necessary, change the directions to suit the particular machine you wish to operate.

Some machines have no ribbers, or they are expensive, and, for personal use, easy to do without. Simulated ribbing will suffice, or a stitch may be dropped and picked up with the tool or crochet hook, the correct way; but I feel that if one wishes to get away from the cheaper machine look, especially around necklines, etc., it is better to rib by hand.

▶ PROJECT ◀

► *See "Answers," page 215 for possible mistakes in fundamentals.*

The body measurements given in many knitting manuals are very confusing. It is not body measurements that are needed for knit design but the necessary measurements of the finished garment for a particular person. No blocking will ever stop a skirt from cupping if the necessary width has not been added at the hips.

The following women's and misses' measurements are those usually seen:

SIZES	12	14	16	18	20
Bust	30	32	34	36	38
Waist	25	26½	28	30	32
Hip	33	35	37	39	41
Arm Length	16½	17	17½	18	18

A size 14 is 32 inches around the bust. It is not a bra measurement that we require. We do not want to stretch to fit, but work to the finished garment measurements. When a designer designs clothes, she adds the necessary

3
Measurements and Stitch Gauge

fullness to suit the requirements of the individual, the style of garment, and the type of material.

TAKING MEASUREMENTS

Never try to take your own measurements.

Waist

There may be difficulty in locating the position of the waist: it is just below the ribs and can be easily located by bending sideways.

In a large figure where the abdomen is raised in the corset, the actual waist is not used in front. Lower the tape a half inch or, if necessary, 1 inch.

This measurement should be taken with two fingers between the body and the tapemeasure. This does not mean that it should be taken loosely, but the tape may be moved around the waist easily, not tightly.

Bust

The position of the bust varies with the individual. It may be two inches below the armpit in young figures, or four inches or more for some adults. This measurement is taken exactly around the fullest part. The tape is not raised at the back. Knitting is worked straight, horizontally.

This measurement is the one used when buying a bra or a pattern and is not the one used for the finished garment. This measurement is taken as a guide for the next two.

To find the necessary bust measurement, the across-the-back underarm measurement and the front bust measurement are required.

Across-the-back underarm

Raise and bend arms slightly toward the front. Do not raise arms too high. Find the mid-point of the hollow which comes immediately under the tip of the shoulder and measure across the back, from hollow to hollow where the underarm seams should be. See Illustration 1.

Front bust measurement

This is taken across the largest part of the bust in a horizontal line from underarm to underarm seam and loose enough to allow flat fingers under the tape.

Total bust measurement

The back and front combined measurements are the necessary total bust measurement. Check this measurement by adding 4 inches to the previous bust measurement, and it will give you the least your combined bust measurement should measure for any knitted sweater.

Under no conditions should the back underarm measurement be larger than the front measurement.

Contrary to belief, on a normal figure there is not a great deal of difference in these measurements, even for a woman. One must allow for freedom of movement at the back.

The combined measurement must be at least 4 inches more than a bra or normal bust measurement, adding 1 inch for B cup, 2 for C, etc., to actual bra measurement.

Waist to underarm

To aid in taking the correct measurement, fasten the tape around the waist. The measurement is taken from the

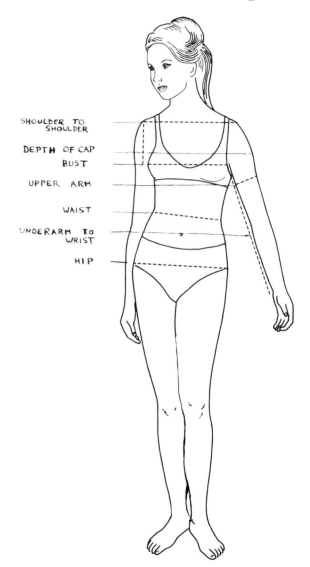

SHOULDER TO SHOULDER
DEPTH OF CAP
BUST
UPPER ARM
WAIST
UNDERARM TO WRIST
HIP

ILLUSTRATION 1

hollow of the armpit (do not raise the arms too high) to the center of the tape around the waist. This would be too long for armholes for fitted caps of sleeves, so deduct 1 inch from this measurement and the deducted measurement is the one used. (No sleeve fits close to the armpit.)

Shoulder to shoulder

I consider this a very important measurement. There is nothing worse than drooping shoulders. Raise an arm and feel the shoulder tip at the very top—just before the slope. Measure across the shoulders at the back from the small bone that marks the tip of one shoulder to the other. See illustration.

When taking a child's shoulder measurement, multiply the inches by two. If the answer is almost the necessary chest measurement, you will know it is too big. There must be sufficient stitches to take off at the underarm.

Wrist

This measurement is taken below the wrist bone toward the hand and is taken exactly.

Upper arm

Because the largest part of the upper arm varies with the individual, measure the fullest part and take it exactly. Do not add anything. This applies to a child too. The width is taken care of when we come to sleeves.

Forearm

This is the fullest part between the wrist and the elbow. It is only necessary for women with large forearms and for men. It should be taken exactly.

Sleeve underarm length

The arm should be raised a little. This measurement is taken from the underarm mid-point, the hollow at the armpit, down the arm to the wrist, on a line with the thumb. One inch is deducted from this measurement, as for the waist to underarm measurement. This is the one used for the sleeve length.

Armhole or armscye

The armhole or armscye is the closed curve starting from the shoulder tip, passing around and under the arm and back to the shoulder tip again. Many armholes, especially in larger, cheaper clothes are too large, giving an ugly fit in front, or they may be too small in garments for smaller sizes, especially if one perspires. Try to take this measurement, then test your ability with the following rule.

An armhole curve should be at least seven or eight inches more than the upper-arm measurement, never less, according to the needs of the wearer. For an adult, this means that if the exact upper-arm measurement is 11 inches, the curve of the armhole must measure 18 or 19 inches. Whether you add 7 or 8 inches is a matter for you to decide.

If the combined back and front bust or chest measurements and the shoulder-to-shoulder measurements are taken correctly, there should only be about 1 inch of stitches to be bound off at the beginning of the armhole shaping, for an adult.

These are all the necessary measurements for the first project, a sweater. In order to test your ability, measure a man, a woman, and a child, and write the answers on the chart.

	Man	Woman	Child
waist			
bust or chest (straight measurement)			
across the back underarm			
front bust or chest measurement			
back and front bust measurements combined			
waist to underarm			
shoulder to shoulder			
wrist			
upper arm			
forearm			
sleeve underarm length			
armhole or armscye			

STITCH GAUGE

The Stitch Gauge is the name given to the number of stitches to the inch and rows to the inch that are measured on a piece of stockinette stitch. The gauge depends upon the material knitted, the size of the needles, and the nature of a person's knitting. An additional factor is the suitable tension of the machine.

So much difficulty has been encountered in the fit of knits partly because of an inaccurate stitch gauge and partly because of not knowing how to take necessary measurements. Both are equally important. Remember, when diagramming, the final necessary measurements are to be used. Therefore, the stitch gauge will be the same as when the garment is worn. Becoming accustomed to the small amount of stretch that the material will have when it is flattened takes practice—but this knack does come with time.

At the beginning, I advise steaming the piece of fabric. This does not mean, however, that it should be pinned down—in which case it could be pinned to many sizes. Simply steam over the piece, on the wrong side, using a damp cloth and a medium hot iron, or no cloth and a steam iron, *keeping the weight of the iron in the hand.* Now it will be the same as the fabric in the completed garment.

Knitting a sample

With the yarn and the needles that are to be used for the garment, cast on 24 stitches and knit a piece of stockinette stitch (knit one row, purl one row) for about 2½ inches. (For thicker material, fewer stitches are necessary: the heavier the yarn, however, the greater the possibility of error.)

METHOD

Use the stockinette stitch for the gauge of any texture stitch. This method is also used when making a gauge on a machine.

► Steam the piece of material.
► Count the number of stitches and rows to the inch, as in the diagram. A linen tape is the best. Do not measure the loops on the needle but in the center of the work. Do this several times, over 1 inch, then 2. Remember, ½ a stitch makes a big difference when measuring stitches to the inch. For example, a piece of material 12 inches long, 6 stitches to the inch, requires 72 stitches. But 12 inches at 6½ stitches to the inch needs 78 stitches—a difference of 6 stitches, which is important in the fit of a garment. See Diagram 13.

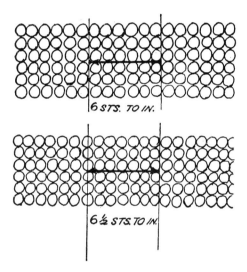

6 STS. TO IN.

6½ STS. TO IN.

DIAGRAM 13

FUNDAMENTALS

For those who prefer to crochet rather than knit, or even like to use both in a garment, the same principles for shaping apply equally well to crochet as to knit. The same method for taking measurements is necessary, and the equivalent amounts are added. The same method for taking the stitch gauge applies as does the need for checking as one proceeds. Generally there are fewer stitches to the inch in crochet, and a mistake would be greater than if one were knitting with medium-weight yarn. In addition, the garment might actually be knitted and then finished or decorated with crochet stitches. An evening sweater could be bedecked gaily with crochet edging; and suits, coats, etc., can be given a distinctive touch with fringe, popcorn- or shell-stitch.

In taking a stitch gauge in crochet, make a sample piece as for knitting, about 3 inches wide and 2 inches long, of the stitch that is to be used for the actual garment.

4
Crochet

When considering the amount of material to use, remember that crochet requires 1½ as much as knitting: That is, if 12 spools of ribbon were used for knitting, approximately 18 spools would be necessary for crochet.

The stitch that gives the most body to the garment is single crochet. Consider the type and weight of the yarn and the purpose of the garment. Single crochet is good for fine materials used in blouses and dresses; heavier material is necessary for coats and also for ribbons.

STITCHES

Single crochet

For single crochet (sc), make a chain the desired length; skip one chain and insert hook from the front into the second chain stitch from the hook; *thread over the hook and draw the thread over the stitch (there are now two loops on the hook); thread over the hook and draw the thread through both loops on the hook; repeat from* in each chain stitch across the row. See Illustration 2.

Double crochet

For double crochet (dc), make a chain the desired length; thread over the hook; then insert it in the 4th stitch from the hook; draw the thread through (3 loops on the hook); thread over the hook and draw through 2 loops (2 loops on the hook); thread over the hook and draw through 2 loops, one loop remaining on the hook. See Illustration 3.

Treble crochet

For treble crochet (tc) chain the desired length; thread over the hook twice; insert the hook in the fifth chain from the hook; draw the thread through (4 loops on the hook). Thread over the hook, draw through 2 loops (3

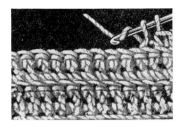

ILLUSTRATION 2

ILLUSTRATION 6

ILLUSTRATION 3

ILLUSTRATION 7

ILLUSTRATION 10

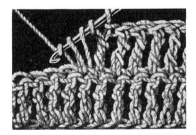

ILLUSTRATION 4

ILLUSTRATION 8

ILLUSTRATION 11

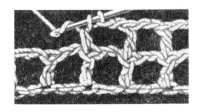

ILLUSTRATION 5

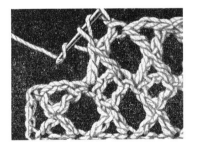

ILLUSTRATION 9

ILLUSTRATION 12

loops on the hook). Thread over the hook and draw through 2 loops (2 loops on the hook). Thread over and pull through remaining 2 loops. See Illustration 4.

Block or mesh

The block, or mesh, is very often used. Work the first double crochet in the 8th chain from the hook;* chain 2; skip 2 stitches; then double crochet in the next stitch; repeat from* to the end of the row. See Illustration 5. For succeeding rows chain 5 to turn.

Block or solid mesh

Four double crochets form a block or solid mesh. Proceed in the same manner as for open mesh, but in every other block work 2 double crochets instead of 2 chain stitches. See Illustration 6.

Slanting shell stitch

For the slanting shell stitch, make the foundation chain; then work two double crochets in the 4th stitch from the hook; skip 3 stitches; slip stitch in the next stitch;* chain 3; 2 double crochets in the same stitch as the slip stitch; skip 3 stitches; slip stitch in the next stitch; repeat from*.

On the 2nd row, chain 3; turn; 2 double crochets in the slip stitch; slip stitch in the 3 chain loop of shell in previous row;* chain 3; 2 double crochets in the same space; slip stitch in the next shell; repeat from*. See Illustration 7.

Bean- or popcorn-stitch

For the bean- or popcorn stitch, work 3 double crochets in the same space; take the hook from the loop and insert in the first double crochet, as in Illustration 8; draw the loop through and chain 1 to tighten the stitch. See Illustration 8.

Cross treble

For cross treble, chain the desired length; thread over the hook twice; insert it in the 5th stitch from the hook;* thread over and through 2 loops; thread over and through 2 loops; thread over; skip 2 stitches; insert in the next stitch and work off all the loops on the needle, 2 stitches at a time; chain 2; double crochet in the center of the stitch to form a cross; thread over twice; insert in the next stitch; and repeat from*. See Illustration 9.

Cluster stitch

For the cluster stitch, work 3 or 4 double or treble crochets in the same stitch, always keeping the last loop of each crochet on the needle; thread over; and pull through all the loops on the hook. See Illustration 10.

Lacet stitch

For the lacet stitch, chain the desired length; work 1 single crochet in the 10 stitch from the hook; chain 3; skip 2 stitches; 1 double crochet in the next stitch;* chain 3; skip 2 stitches; 1 single crochet in the next stitch; chain 3; skip 2 stitches; 1 double crochet in the next stitch; repeat from* to the end of the row.

On the second row, chain 8; double crochet in double crochet;* chain 5; double crochet in the next double crochet; repeat from* to the end of the row. See Illustration 11.

Lover's-knot stitch

For the lover's-knot stitch, chain for the desired length;* draw a ¼ inch loop on the hook; thread over and pull through the chain; single crochet through the back strand of the elongated loop; draw another ¼ inch loop; single crochet into the loop; skip 4 stitches; single crochet into the next stitch, repeat from*.

To turn, make ⅜ inch knots;* work 1-inch single crochet through the first loose knot of the previous row; draw up a ¼ inch loop on the hook; thread over and pull through the chain; single crochet through the back strand of the elongated loop; draw a second loop up ¼ inch; single crochet in this loop; single crochet in the next loose knot; repeat from* across the row and end with 1 single crochet in last loose knot; repeat this row throughout. See Illustration 12.

Note that when crocheting, there are certain rules for turning the work, or having the necessary number of chain stitches.

For single crochet (sc):	Chain 4 to turn.
For double crochet (dc):	Chain 3 to turn.
For treble crochet (tr):	Chain 1 to turn.

The number of chains takes the place of the first stitch of the row.

5
Ribbon Knits

We must thank a group of Parisian designers who originated knitting with ribbon and discovered its durability, versatility and elegance. It is remarkable how the different types of ribbon with their silky finish lend themselves to a variety of textures and patterns and are adaptable for all occasions—for business, for the cocktail hour, and the ballroom. If you are one of the lucky ones and have a ribbon sheath or suit in your wardrobe, you know the pleasure and satisfaction of wearing one of the most luxurious, most crease-resistant packables.

The actual cost of the material is a mere fraction of a finished garment made of material of similar calibre. By making your own ribbon-knit, you can achieve that envied couturier look that is so very, very expensive— and only available at elite stores or exclusive boutiques.

Today there are several types of ribbon used for ribbon knits. There are rayon, rayon and silk combined, rayon and silk with a metallic thread through the center, and all-silk organdy ribbon. Some have woven, others have fused edges.

Knitting with ribbon takes practice, since it is quite different from ordinary knitting, but once the technique is acquired, a garment may be made more quickly than with other materials (excluding, of course, bulky knits). Large needles are used, so fewer stitches are necessary. I do, however, consider ribbon knits to be exacting to make in their knitting, blocking, finishing, and final pressing.

FUNDAMENTALS

The ribbon should be kept flat on the needle and worked very loosely, allowing considerable slack. So there will be no strain, unwind the ribbon a couple of yards each time—do not pull out too much, or it will curl. I have found that holding the spool at the ends between the thumb and index finger of the right hand and drawing the ribbon out with the left hand helps to keep it flat.

Ribbon, linen, and cotton thread should not be knitted in plain stockinette stitch; because, for some unknown reason, the tension draws the stitches, and they form diagonally, not straight up and down. This is why for plain ribbon-knitting, one always knits in the back of the knit stitch, unless otherwise stated in the directions.

Remember that the ribbon must be held flat so that each stitch comes off the needle uncrushed. The ribbon should always remain in the same position over the index finger, either left or right, whether one knits in the Continental or English way: one reason (among others) why, when first learning to knit, one should not keep throwing the thread over the needle with the hand.

STITCHES

Always identify one side of the ribbon by marking it with a pencil or with chalk. This is the side that should be against the needle, and the marking will help you to keep it in position. Large needles are used, #8 to #10, and you should obtain anywhere from 4 to 5½ stitches per inch. See Illustration 13.

Twisted stockinette stitch

For the knit side, use the method that follows.

METHOD

1. Insert the right-hand needle through the back of the stitch on the left-hand needle. The dark side is the marked side. See Illustration 14.
2. Place the ribbon over the needle from the back to the front, as in ordinary knitting. See Illustration 15.
3. Pull the loop through; then slip the stitch off the left-hand needle. Note the marked side of the ribbon. See Illustration 16.
4. Continue to the end of the row.

ILLUSTRATION 13

ILLUSTRATION 14

ILLUSTRATION 15

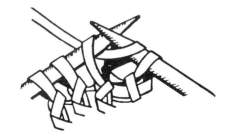

ILLUSTRATION 16

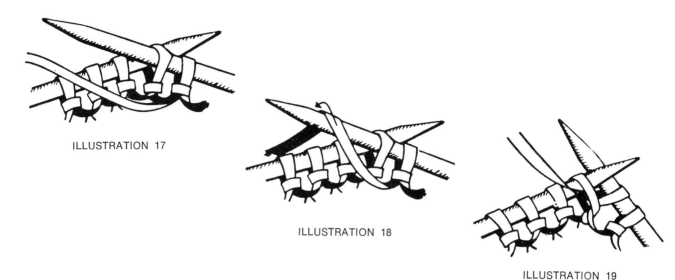

ILLUSTRATION 17

ILLUSTRATION 18

ILLUSTRATION 19

ILLUSTRATION 20

For the purl side, use the method that follows.

METHOD

1. Insert the needle from right to left in front of the stitch, like ordinary purling. See Illustration 17.

2. Place the ribbon over the needle from the front to the back. See Illustration 18.

3. Pull the loop through; then slip the stitch off the left-hand needle. See Illustration 19.

4. Continue to the end of the row.

Woven stitch

The difference between the twisted stockinette stitch and the woven stitch is that the yarn is thrown differently both for the knit and the purl. See Illustration 20.

For the knit side, use the method that follows.

ILLUSTRATION 21

ILLUSTRATION 22

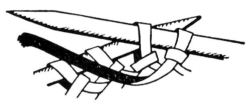

ILLUSTRATION 23

METHOD

1. Insert the right-hand needle through the back of the stitch on the left-hand needle. See Illustration 21.

2. Place the ribbon over the needle from the front to the back. See Illustration 22.

3. Pull the loop through; then slip the stitch off the left-hand needle. See Illustration 23.

4. Continue to the end of the row.

For the purl side, use the method that follows.

ILLUSTRATION 24

METHOD

1. Insert the needle from the right to the left in the front of the stitch. See Illustration 24.

2. Place the ribbon over the needle from the back to the front. See Illustration 25.

3. Pull the loop through; then slip the stitch off the left-hand needle. See Illustration 26.

4. Continue to the end of the row.

If the pattern appears irregular, do not pull the stitch lengthwise. Place the knitting needle or crochet hook under the stitches and pull gently.

ILLUSTRATION 25

ILLUSTRATION 26

Yarn and ribbon

Often yarn is used with ribbon. Sometimes there are two rows of ribbon and two rows of yarn, which may vary from looped, or nubby, to very fine yarn or thread of wool and rayon, or partly cotton or linen; metallic threads may also be combined. One may also have narrow stripes of yarn and wider ones of ribbon and vice versa.

For a good stitch using ribbon and yarn, use the following method:

METHOD

Row 1 (ribbon): * K. 1, bring the ribbon to the front, slip a stitch, as if to purl. Take the ribbon to the back. * Repeat.
Row 2 (ribbon): Purl back.
Row 3 (yarn or thread): Knit.
Row 4 (yarn or thread): Purl.
Repeat the four rows.

Using two sizes of needles

Occasionally two sizes of needles are used, say number 13 and number 4. This gives a long stitch and resembles hairpin lace.

METHOD

Row 1: Using size 13 needles, knit in the back of the stitch, placing the ribbon over the needle from the back to the front.
Row 2: Using size 4 needles, knit across.

STITCH GAUGE

The gauge may be from 4 to 5½ stitches to the inch, depending upon the needles (generally size 8 to 10), the type of ribbon, and stitch used. Only 14 to 18 stitches are necessary for a gauge, and the ribbon must be steamed and pressed. The stitches should not be stretched, but actually pushed closely together. This is better done with a steam iron, over a lightweight cloth, (organdy is good) on the right side, using the steam and a slight pressure to flatten the stitches. Press a little at a time with the tip of the iron, being careful to use the right temperature for the material. Be sure to keep the correct width when measuring.

Since skirts made of rayon ribbon have a tendency to be a little weighty, 2 or 3 inches should be allowed for stretch in length, according to the type of skirt and the amount of material used. This is also due to the properties of rayon. It does stretch. Silk is not stretchy; therefore only allow about 1 inch.

By this time, you should have decided what type of basic sweater you wish to knit, or diagram, if you are busy. Use a sketch, a photograph, or visualize the style. It must be a *basic* sweater, not an evening one fitted at the sides. These come later. This is a learning process, and no matter how adept you are at knitting, use ribbing and stockinette stitch for the back of the sweater. No fancy stitches. Knit from your diagram. The main considerations are that your lines be clear and your figures accurate. No written explanations are necessary.

If you do not own a yarn shop, buy your material from a reputable store. The knitting manuals for a given brand will tell you the amount of yarn and size of needles. There are many "no dye lot" sweater yarns on the market, and I suggest these, because one need not buy all at one time: If one intends to go into business, the ability to re-order is a good selling point.

Use the following instructions to diagram and chart any size slipover or cardigan, with any type of yarn.

6
Slipover Sweaters and Cardigans

Slipover sweater

Diagramming and charting. Simple sweaters are made the same width at the front as the back, unless the person has an unusually large bust. (A woman with a large bust, however, should never wear a slipover sweater.)

Two sets of different-sized needles are not necessary for knitting a sweater: It is advisable to increase at the waist rather than use needles two sizes larger. If smaller needles are desired for the ribbing, however, make a stitch gauge with the larger ones and figure the number of stitches necessary for the bust; then use the same number of stitches with the smaller needles for the ribbing.

Your work should be knitted neither too tightly nor too loosely. Knitted sweaters should be washable. If knitted too loosely, they sag; if fitted too tightly, they mat.

The following woman's measurements are the ones we shall use for the examples throughout the sweater lessons.

Waist	28 inches
Across the Back Underarm	17½ "
Front Bust Measurement	18½ "
Total Bust Measurement	36 "
Wrist	6 "
Upper arm	11 "
Forearm	9 "
Sleeve Underarm Length	18 "
Armhole or Armscye	18 "

Stitch Gauge—6 stitches to the inch
8 rows to the inch

EXAMPLE

1. Waistband or ribbing—worn below the waist:

The waist is 28 inches. Half of this is 14 inches to be

multiplied by the stitch gauge, 6 stitches to the inch.
14 times 6 is 84 stitches, which is divisible by 4, for K. 2,
P. 2. If not divisible by 4, take the nearest number that
is. Whether to use K. 2, P. 2, or K. 1, P. 1, depends upon
the type of yarn. For heavier yarn, use K. 2, P. 2, but it
is advisable that a beginner always knit K. 2, P. 2, for
ribbing. The ribbing is generally 3 inches or more for
adults, and 2 inches for a child. Be sure to stretch to the
correct width before measuring. See Diagram 14.

2. Body of the sweater:

The fronts and backs of basic sweaters are always the
same width.

The necessary bust measurement is 36 inches; ½ of
36 is 18 inches; 18 × 6 stitches to the inch is 108 stitches.

Adding stitches. In basic sweaters, all the stitches are
added on the first row after the ribbing, and added evenly
across the row on the right side of the work. The same
principies apply to a man's, woman's, or child's sweater.

METHOD

▶ ½ the waist measurement multiplied by the stitch
gauge is the number of stitches for ½ the waist.
▶ ½ the bust or chest measurement multiplied by the
stitch gauge gives the number of stitches for across the
back.
▶ The difference between the stitches for ½ the bust
and ½ the waist equals the number of stitches to be
added.

EXAMPLE

▶ The number of stitches for ½ the waist is 84 stitches,
and ½ the bust is 108 stitches, a difference of 24 stitches.
▶ Take the number of stitches to be added into the
number of stitches to be increased: for example, to add
12 stitches to 72—12 into 72 goes 6 times. Increase,

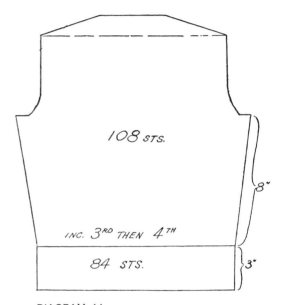

DIAGRAM 14

therefore, in every 6th stitch. If the number does not go in evenly, do not increase in the stitches that are left over.

► In our example, we divide 24 into 84 which goes 3½ times, or 2 in 7 stitches; so, we increase first in the 3rd stitch, then in the 4th across the row and purl back. Work stockinette stitch for 8 inches, which is the underarm to waist measurement.

▶ PROJECT ◀

► *Diagram and chart your own sample sweater to the armhole.*

► *Knit your own sweater to the armhole.*

On a machine, binding off is much more difficult and time-consuming than adding stitches. It is, therefore, easier to begin at the top and knit down. For this reason, wait until you understand all the back shaping before you begin, or try both ways to test the time and ease.

Cardigan or coat-sweater

Diagramming and charting. As with the slipover, the following instructions may be used for diagramming and charting any size.

► A simple cardigan or coat-sweater is knitted straight to the underarm, using half the bust or chest measurement for the back. If the hips are larger than the chest measurement, for example, 46 inches for the hips and 42 inches for the chest, a medium measurement should be used—44 inches. No cardigan should be larger at the hips than at the chest.

► A narrow band should be used at the bottom of a cardigan, about one and one-half inches wide, or, actually, it should be the front-band width, unless you are making a sweater that fits at the waist. A wide band gives added width at the hips. The band may be of K. 1, P. 1, garter stitch, seed stitch, etc.

► The length of a cardigan depends upon the figure of the wearer. It should not stop just above a protruding bottom. Mark the proposed length and stand back for judgment: The sweater should not be too long for a short person, since she would appear to be all body; and it should not be too long for a tall person, since she would appear to be even taller.

► Diagram 15 is self-explanatory.

If you wish to have experience in diagramming and charting both a slipover and a cardigan, use the following measurements. They are not standard but are a man's and woman's measurements, taken as they should be for knitting or crochet. Few of us are a perfect 12 or 14. We must learn to cope with the irregularities of form, so that the garments are not too tight in one place or too large in another.

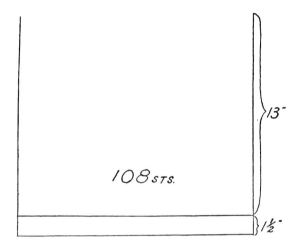

DIAGRAM 15

	MAN	WOMAN
Waist	38 inches	28 inches
Across Back Underarm	21 "	17½ "
Front Bust or Chest	21 "	18½ "
Chest or Bust	42 "	36 "
Waist to Underarm	11 "	8 "
Shoulder to Shoulder	17 "	14½ "
Wrist	8 "	6 "
Upper arm	13 "	11 "
Sleeve Underarm Length	20 "	17½ "
Armhole or Armscye	21 "	19 "

Gauge—6 stitches to the inch—man
7 stitches to the inch—woman

In all diagramming and charting, no graph paper is necessary. Become accustomed to drawing diagrams. They may look very amateurish at first, but you will be surprised how you will progress with a little determination. Think that nothing is impossible if you make up your mind.

▶ *PROWJECTS* ◀

► *Diagram and chart to the armhole: the back of the man's slipover and cardigan.*

► *Diagram and chart to the armhole: the back of the woman's slipover and cardigan. (You may wonder why you are diagramming both slipover and cardigan, when they have apparently the same figures. There is a reason, which we shall learn later.)*

► *Check your answers on pages 216 to 217.*

ARMHOLES

Not too many years ago the shaping of an armhole was a complicated procedure. Fashion design today is much more simple, yet beautiful. One might compare modern dress design with modern furniture design—functional, simple, and of easy construction.

I wonder if you have noticed that many armholes in knits are too small. From actual experience, I have learned that a 10-inch to a 12-inch upper arm is the average size of a young adult; for many older women, however, the size is greater. Naturally, the size of the armhole should always be proportionate to the size of the upper arm.

Throughout the course, when considering the differences for a child, allow ¾ of what was considered for an adult; therefore, 5½ to 6 inches should be added to the upper arm for a child's armhole curve.

7
Shaping of Armholes and Shoulders

Measurements

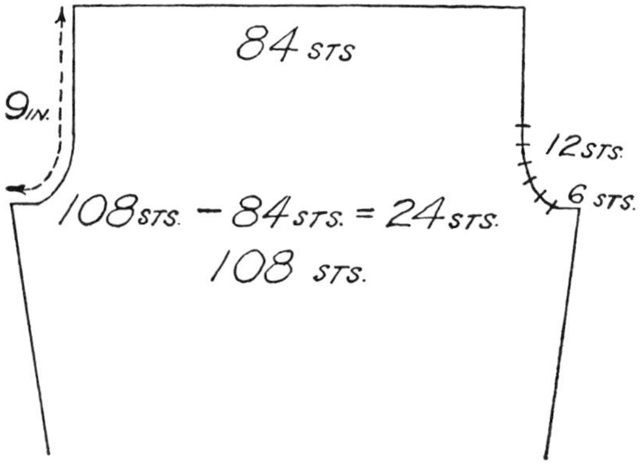

A 10-inch upper arm requires from 17 to 18 inches for the armhole curve—fitted cap.

An 11-inch upper arm requires from 18 to 19 inches for the armhole curve—fitted cap.

A 12-inch upper arm requires from 19 to 20 inches for the armhole curve—fitted cap,

and so on for larger upper arms.

If the total armhole measurement is 18 inches, half the armhole curve is 9 inches, measuring around the curve to the tip of the shoulder.

Shaping

Follow Diagrams 16 and 17. The shoulder to shoulder measurement is 14 inches; 14 times 6 stitches to the inch is 84 stitches. This is an even number. Make it even if it does not work out that way. Always use even numbers in knitting.

The difference between the stitches required for the shoulder, 84 stitches, and the number of stitches for the across the back underarm, 108 stitches, is 24 stitches, to be taken off at both sides of the armholes—12 stitches to be taken off for each. We bind off half the total number of stitches at the beginning, then the remainder are reduced by knitting 2 together at the beginning and end of every front row.

Since we can only bind off at the beginning of rows, we bind off half of the 12 stitches, which is 6 stitches, at the beginning of the next two rows, then knit 2 together at the beginning and end of the next 6 knitted rows, until the shoulder stitches remain, 84 stitches.

Work even in stockinette stitch until half the armhole measurement is knitted, which is 9 inches, measuring around.

If the **number** is uneven divide the number by 2 and

DIAGRAM 16

allow the extra stitch to be bound off at first—8 stitches bound off and knit 2 together, 7 times.

On a machine, it is sometimes impossible to measure around, so take ½ the total measurement for a man or a woman and deduct 1½ inches, for a child, 1 to 1¼ inches straight from the first bind off; then count the number of rows per inch.

METHOD

1. Bind off ½ the total number of stitches at the beginning of the next 2 rows, then knit 2 together at the beginning and end of the knitted rows, until the total number of stitches has been reduced.

2. Work even until ½ the armhole measurement is knitted.

▶ PROJECTS ◀

► Diagram and chart the armholes of the 4 examples on pages 217 and 218.
► Diagram your own sweater to the tip of the shoulder, ready for the shaping of the shoulders.
► Check the answers on pages 217 and 218.

SHOULDERS

The correct fit of shoulders has a great effect upon the fit of the upper part of the sleeves, the neckline, and the bust. I suggest for knits that you never create anything extreme, always having a shoulder line that suits the individual.

Shaping

Shoulder lines are sloped to conform to the shape of the shoulder. Allow one-third of the total number of shoulder

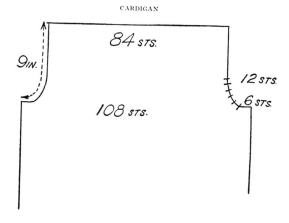

CARDIGAN

DIAGRAM 17

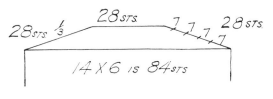

DIAGRAM 18

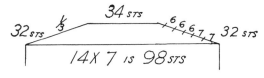

DIAGRAM 19

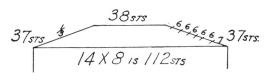

DIAGRAM 20

to shoulder stitches for each shoulder and one-third for the back of the neck. Never have fewer stitches for the back of the neck than the shoulder.

Follow Diagram 18; one-third of 84 stitches is 28 stitches for each shoulder and 28 stitches for the back of the neck.

A few explanations are necessary, so that you understand why so many steps are used for certain stitch gauges. Strange as it may seem, women's shoulders are straighter and broader than they were twenty years ago. A slope of about one inch is the best for all purposes.

The following stitch gauges may be used for the shaping:

For 6 stitches to the inch there are 8 rows to the inch.
For 7 stitches to the inch there are 10 rows to the inch.
For 8 stitches to the inch there are 12 rows to the inch, etc.

Because we are only able to bind off at the beginning of rows, and 6 stitches to the inch has 8 rows, half of the 8 rows, 4, must be the number of times we are able to bind off at one end and 4 times at the other. For 7 stitches to the inch, there are 10 rows, so 5 is the number of times that we bind off the allotted stitches for the shoulder. 8 stitches to the inch, which have 12 rows, require 6. Follow diagrams.

If the stitch gauge is 6½ stitches to the inch, I would consider it 7 and use 5 slopes for each shoulder.

If the number does not go evenly into the stitches for the shoulder, allow the extra stitches for the slopes nearest the shoulder.

In Diagram 18, the stitch gauge is 6 stitches to the inch, so 28 is divided by 4, which means that 7 stitches are bound off, 4 times on each shoulder, making 8 rows altogether.

METHOD

► One-third of the stitches is used for each shoulder, and one-third for the back of the neck.

► Shape each shoulder in from 3 to 7 slopes, depending upon the stitch gauge.

5 stitches to the inch	3 slopes
6 stitches to the inch	4 "
7 stitches to the inch	5 "
8 stitches to the inch	6 "

When the stitch gauge is 5 stitches to the inch or under, deduct 1 inch of stitches from each of the last slopes and add the 2 inches to the back of the neck stitches. The neck opening would be too large if the last slope were used.

► Note carefully that for a high, round neckline slipover, without any opening—also referring to a turtle neck—the one-third neck opening is not large enough for the head to pass through, so do not bind off the last step on each side but add these stitches to the back of the neck. Study diagrams carefully.

► When working from the top down, figure the back using the following measurements. See Diagram 18.

This method is easier for machine-knitters.

Waist—28 inches.
Bust—36 inches.
Underarm to Waist—8 inches.
Shoulder to Shoulder—14 inches.
Armhole—18 inches.
Stitch gauge or tension—6 stitches to the inch,
8 rows to the inch.

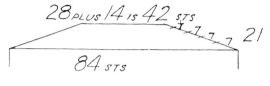

DIAGRAM 21

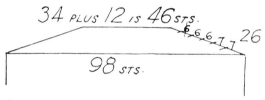

DIAGRAM 22

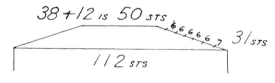

DIAGRAM 23

EXAMPLE

► For either a cardigan or slipover, except for a high round neck, cast on 28 stitches for the back of the neck. For a high round-neck slipover, cast on 28 stitches plus 2 times 7, which is 14, making 42 stitches. Add 7 stitches at each end, every other row, until 84 stitches. Work even until the shaping for the armhole. 7½ inches × 8 rows to the inch equals 60 rows. But the diagram shows 6 decreases of knit 2 together, every other row, making 12 rows. 60 rows minus 12 rows is 48 rows. Therefore work 48 rows even, then shape the armholes, until 108 stitches.

► The underarm to waist is 8 inches, at 8 rows to the inch is 64 rows to the waist.

► For the ribbing, decrease to 84 stitches, or change the tension, or place the stitches on straight needles and work by hand.

▶ PROJECT ◀

► *Diagram and chart the shoulders of the man's and woman's example sweaters as follows:*

Slipover sweater: shoulders for either a V, square, or oval neckline.
Slipover sweater: shoulders for high, round neckline.
Cardigan: shoulders for cardigan of general styling.
Test your answers on page 219.

BACK OPENINGS

Do you understand the method of shaping so far? You should not pass to the next step unless the preceding steps are clear in your mind.

Back openings are very stylish for certain figures (straight backs) but they should be taboo for older persons, especially if one has a "dowager's hump," as it is called. Such adornments as openings attract attention; and any figure discrepancies should be camouflaged, if possible, not pointed out.

Hand-knitting

An opening generally begins immediately after the stitches for the armhole have been decreased, or approximately two inches up from the first bind off.

METHOD

   1. Knit across to the center.

8
Backs of Sweaters

2. Place the remaining half of the stitches on a stitch holder or a safety-pin. The back is worked in two separate pieces.

3. Continue the right side until the tip of the shoulder is reached.

4. Shape the shoulder and neckline.

5. The left side is completed in the same way as the right, but in reverse.

6. The opening may be single crocheted, with loops of chain stitch used as buttonholes. This is done after the garment is put together.

All change of shaping is done on the right side of the work with the exception of binding off, which cannot be done at the end of a row. It is important to remember, therefore, that this, and only this, is done on the wrong side of the work. The knit-2-together decreases are always worked on the right side at the very edge; and if these rules are remembered, no confusion can arise either at the armholes, shoulders, necklines, or, indeed, anywhere on the garment.

Machine knitting

In order to work the 2 pieces separately and at the same time, 2 balls of yarn are necessary. To start the opening at the back, use the following method:

METHOD

1. Knit across to the center.

2. Use the second ball for the other half, and work back and forth on both sides until the tips of the shoulders are reached.

3. Bind off the left shoulder in the same way as the right, in reverse.

4. Bind off all the stitches for the back of the neck.

FULL-FASHIONED SWEATERS

The word full-fashioned, with regard to sweaters, is very misleading. It simply means that the decreases show both on the armholes and caps of the sleeves. Strictly, from the point of view of design, this technique is not correct, because, by rights, any change of shaping takes place in the seam—Whoever thought of drawing attention to a seam in a sewn garment? Also, there should be a certain number of stitches bound off at the underarm. All garment shaping should conform to the contour of the body. If one does wish to achieve a full-fashioned effect, however, find the number of stitches that are to be decreased, the same as previously, then decrease by knitting 2 together, at the beginning and end of every fourth row, 5 stitches in, until all the necessary stitches have been reduced.

COMPLETING THE BACK OF THE NECK

Slipover sweaters

For slipover sweaters without an opening either at the front or at the back, do not bind off the back of the neck, no matter what type of neckline in front, if ribbing is to be used around the neckline.

If ribbing is desired, knit the same rib as for the waist. (One would never put two different designs of lace on a blouse.) Work in K. 2, P. 2, or K. 1, P. 1, as the case may be. One inch is generally the width. Be sure to bind off loosely (to be as elastic as the rest of the work) knitting the knits, and purling the purls, as you bind off.

Cardigans or coat-sweaters

Round necklines. The back of the neck is bound off loosely and the stitches picked up all around the neckline after the sweater is put together.

V-necklines. The same band that is used up the front is continued around the neck; then the ends are woven together either at the back of the neck or at a shoulder seam.

Stitch gauge

Check the stitch gauge of your completed back. Is it the same as when you started? An experienced knitter will not change, but a beginner's gauge must be checked.

Generally, a beginning knitter knits tighter as she progresses, because she gradually learns to throw her thread correctly. Thus the stitch gauge should be checked toward the armhole, if possible. If she has tightened her work, figure the necessary number of stitches from her new gauge for the shoulders. It is so important that shoulders fit.

To learn the necessary number of stitches for the front bust measurement, see the following example:

MEASUREMENTS

    Bust—38 inches.
    First stitch gauge—6½ stitches to the inch.
    Second stitch gauge—7 stitches to the inch.

EXAMPLE

1. Multiply the total bust measurement by the new gauge: 38 times 7 stitches to the inch is 266 stitches.

2. 19 inches times 6½ stitches is 124 stitches for the back.

3. Subtract the back stitches from the total stitches, which is 142 for the front bust.

▶ PROJECT ◀

▶ *Diagram the shoulders of your own sweater and complete the back according to the type desired.*

SLIPOVER

The front of a slipover is knitted in the same way as the back until the front neckline is reached. The extra length that is sometimes added to the section from underarm to waist in front for a woman takes the place of a dart, which is often used when sewing. In knitting, it is eased into the seam, 2 to 4 inches below the underarm. For general purposes, extra length is not necessary, but use your own discretion as to whether ½ inch or 1 inch should be added.

CARDIGAN

Since the position of the buttonholes is important, the side on which the buttons are fastened is knitted first. Therefore, for a woman's garment, it is the left side and for a man's, the right. The general rule for the width of the bands is that they should be at least twice the width

9
Fronts of Sweaters

of the number of stitches required for the buttonhole, more if desired. Place the button on the stockinette stitch to count the number of necessary stitches. The buttonhole should not be in the center of the band. Allow one or two extra stitches toward the edge. For example, in an 8-stitch band using 4 stitches for the buttonhole, 3 stitches should be used at the outside edge, so that when the cardigan is fastened, the button will not jut over the side.

To figure the number of stitches necessary for the cardigan front, take half the total number of stitches required for the back, plus half the number of stitches necessary for the width of each band.

Bands

Because the bands coming up the front only overlap once, it is necessary to add only half the required band stitches on each side, but knit a whole band of a special stitch, if you are not using stockinette stitch, which should be strengthened with ribbon.

EXAMPLE

▶ Follow Diagram 24 for front of cardigan.
▶ In the example given, there are 108 stitches across the back. One-half of 108 stitches is 54 to the center front.
▶ An 8-stitch band is being used; therefore, add half the width of the band, 4 stitches, which equals 58 stitches, 8 of these knitted in band-stitches, and 50 stitches in stockinette, or any texture stitch.
▶ This applies to both sides.
▶ No extra stitches are added for zippers. Either single-crochet the edges or use garter-stitch at the front opening for 3 or 4 stitches.

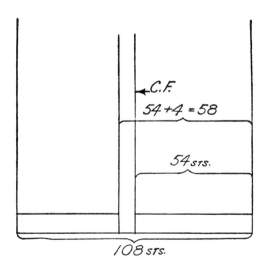

DIAGRAM 24

Pockets

Position. The position of the pockets is important in any garment. There is a general rule that can be applied, whether the pocket is breast, jacket, coat, or sweater pocket, in terms of the location from the seam to the center front.

METHOD

1. Figure the desired width of the pocket from the stitch gauge. An average woman's pocket is 4 inches wide; average man's is 5 inches.
2. Subtract the necessary number of stitches for the pocket from the underarm to center-front stitches. See Diagram 25.
3. Divide the remaining stitches into one-third, allowing two-thirds to the center-front and one-third toward the underarm seam.

EXAMPLE

1. The pocket is 5 inches wide, and there are 6 stitches to the inch: 5 times 6 is 30 stitches for the pocket.
2. 30 stitches from 54 stitches to the center front is 24 stitches.
3. Dividing into one-third, 16 stitches to the center front and 8 stitches to the underarm seam. See Diagram 25.

Note that the depth of a pocket should be equal to the width or longer. The lower edge of the pocket in a cardigan should reach the top of the border.

And openings for breast pockets should be about 2 inches from the first bind-off at the armhole.

Binding off. To bind off, use the following method.

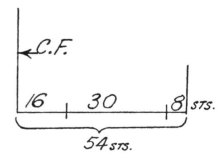

DIAGRAM 25

METHOD

1. Bind off the stitches for the pocket on the right side, the same as for a buttonhole.

2. Knit a piece of stockinette stitch, using the same number of stitches as were bound off, and finish on a knit row.

3. When purling back, use the stitches in the small piece to take the place of those that were bound off. This is the back of the pocket which is sewn down later.

4. Make a big buttonhole, then pick up the stitches afterward and knit down. This makes a firmer pocket.

▶ *PROJECTS* ◀

► *Diagram and chart the fronts of a woman's and man's cardigan to the armholes, placing the position of the pockets.*

► *Diagram and chart your own sweater to the armholes.*

► *Check the answers on pages 220 and 221.*

The neckline of any garment is of the utmost importance and should be designed to be in harmony with the shape of the face and chin and the length of the throat. The general proportions of the body also should be taken into consideration.

A tall, slender person, as a rule, has a long, thin neck, but this is not always the case. A long, pointed neckline will exaggerate the length and thinness of the neck on a tall person, as does a collarless garment. Shallow necklines with high, fitted up-at-the-back collars, as well as rolled collars, are also good for a person with a long neck—and, in addition, excellent for concealing a "dowager's hump." Shallow necklines, whether they are round, square, or high oval, make the neck look shorter.

Consideration must also be given, however, to the contours of the face and chin. A square neckline should never be used with a square jaw because it repeats the same line, whereas a fairly deep oval will detract from the squareness. A pointed chin looks well in a high, round neckline but appears more pointed in a V-neckline.

10
Necklines

High, tight collars are generally trying to plump persons. On the other hand, long, pointed necklines will modify roundness in a full face; and flat collars that carry the line down are good for a short, thick neck.

A broad collar or lapels that carry the eye across the shoulders make a person look broader; on the other hand, a collar or lapels that carry the eye down toward the waist have a tendency to make a person appear longer-waisted. For this reason, long lapels tend to slim the heavy figure.

For older persons, high necklines, or low ones that reveal the generally preserved skin of the upper chest, are good. Sagging, tell-tale chin wrinkles are often concealed by means of a scarf, ribbon with bow, or with a brooch or pin.

After having decided upon the most suitable neckline, the next step is to determine the lowest depth in front.

METHOD

► Place the tapemeasure horizontally from armscye to armscye at the point where the shaping should be begun, remembering that if ribbing is going to be added for sweaters, one inch lower is necessary.

► Now measure the distance from the tip of the shoulder. That means that if the neckline is to be started 4 inches below the tip of the shoulder (no matter what type) and half the armhole measurement is 10 inches, the neckline is begun when 6 inches of the armhole are knitted, measuring the curve.

HIGH, ROUND NECKLINES

Note in the examples that one-third of the shoulder stitches are to be used for the back of the neck.

Slipover with an opening (turtleneck)

A high, round neckline should reach the hollow of the throat, which is generally 2 inches below the tip of the shoulder in front for an adult and 1½ inches for a child. Follow Diagram 26.

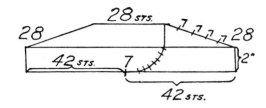

DIAGRAM 26

METHOD

1. High, round necklines begin 2 inches below the tip of the shoulder for an adult, 1½ inches for a child.
2. Knit to half the total shoulder to shoulder stitches, place the other half on a stitch-holder.
3. Subtract the shoulder stitches from the number of stitches to the center front.
4. Shaping: same as for armhole. Bind off half the total number of stitches at the center front, then knit 2 together every front row, until the shoulder stitches remain.
5. Work the shoulder to correspond with the back.
6. Knit the other side to correspond, only in reverse.

EXAMPLE

1. Knit the armhole 2 inches shorter than the back, which is 8 inches.
2. Knit across to half the total number of the shoulder-to-shoulder stitches—42—and place the remaining 42 stitches on a stitch-holder or safety pin. Half the neckline is worked at one time.
3. 42 stitches to the center front. 28 stitches required for the shoulder. 42 stitches minus 28 stitches equals 14 stitches to take off for half the neckline.
4. The shaping of a round neckline is the same as the shaping of an armhole. Bind off half the total number of stitches at the beginning, then knit 2 together, every

other row; that is, bind off 7 stitches at the neck edge, then knit 2 together, every other row, 7 times.

5. Work the shoulder to correspond with the back shoulder.

6. Complete the other side to correspond, but reverse the shaping.

If the armhole is not the same length as the back, knit even until the measurement is reached.

Slipover without opening

METHOD

1. Do not work the last slope of each shoulder.

2. Continue as outlined for the high, round-necked slipover with opening, subtracting the adjusted shoulder measurement from half the total shoulder to shoulder measurement for the number of stitches to be decreased at the neck edge.

Follow Diagram 27.

The last step on both sides of the shoulder is not bound off, as explained in the previous lesson; therefore, there are 21 stitches for each shoulder and 28 plus 14 stitches for the back of the neck.

EXAMPLE

1. Work to the center of the total shoulder-to-shoulder stitches—84 stitches. This is 42 stitches.

2. 42 stitches minus 21 stitches for the shoulder is 21 stitches for half the neckline.

3. Using the same rule as above, half the stitches are bound off at the center front—11 stitches.

4. Then knit 2 together, 10 times, every other row.

If the stitches are not completely decreased when the

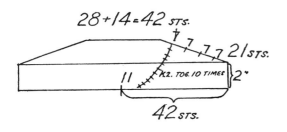

DIAGRAM 27

armhole measurement is reached, knit 2 together at the neck edge, at the same time as decreasing for the shoulders.

High, round-necked cardigan

It is important to remember when figuring for a cardigan that all necklines, except square necklines, are charted from the center front. Follow Diagram 28.

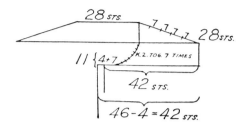

DIAGRAM 28

METHOD

▶ Subtract half the width of the band first. Proceed as with the slipover, adding half the band stitches to the first bind-off.

EXAMPLE

1. The total number of stitches for half the front, after the armholes have been shaped, is 46 stitches minus half the width of the band, 4 stitches (to figure from the center front)—42 stitches.
2. 42 stitches minus 28 stitches for the shoulder equals 14 stitches, which is 7 stitches for the first bind-off, and knit 2 together, 7 times.
3. Half the width of the band is to be added to the first bind-off. 7 stitches plus 4 stitches is 11 stitches, and knit 2 together, 7 times, on every front row.

V-NECKLINES

V-necklines are centered the same way as round necklines; so work to the center front. The main thing to remember is to decrease until the required number of stitches for the shoulder is left. The method of decreasing may be worked out exactly according to rows and the number of stitches to de decreased; but generally the following steps will suffice:

METHOD

1. After the stitches have been bound off at the armhole, or 2 inches from the first bind-off, knit 2 together, every front row, that is every 2nd row, until the shoulder stitches remain. See Diagram 29.

2. At the first bind-off at the armhole, knit 2 together, every 2nd front row, that is, every 4th row, until the shoulder stitches remain. See Diagram 30.

3. Just above the waistline, knit 2 together every 8th row. See Diagram 31.

(On a machine, use 2 balls of yarn and work the left side at the same time as the right, in reverse.)

V-necklines for cardigans

The same decreases apply to cardigans, except that the decreases come inside the bands. The best method is to use the knit-2-together decrease for the left side and the decrease of slip, knit, and pass, for the right.

Also, leave the number of stitches for the band, plus the stitches necessary for the shoulder, so that the band stitches may be knitted around to the center back or a shoulder seam, where they may be joined.

SQUARE NECKLINES

Follow Diagram 32. It is self-explanatory.

Bind off the center stitches and work the left front first, knitting straight to the tip of the shoulder, then shape the shoulder. Attach the yarn and work the right side to correspond, only in reverse.

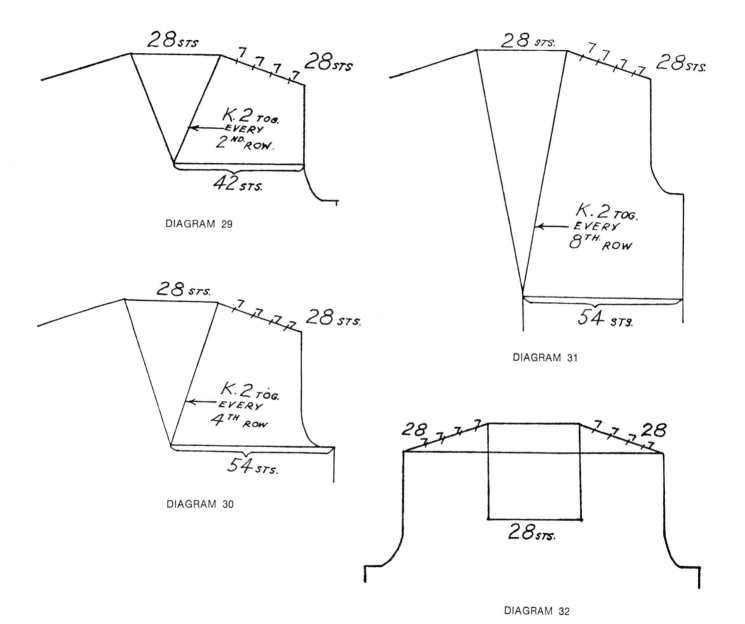

28 sts.   7 7 7 7   28 sts.

K. 2 TOG.
EVERY
2ND. ROW.

42 STS.

DIAGRAM 29

28 sts.   7 7 7 7   28 sts.

K. 2 TOG.
EVERY
4TH ROW

54 STS.

DIAGRAM 30

28 sts.   7 7 7 7   28 sts.

K. 2 TOG.
EVERY
8TH. ROW

54 STS.

DIAGRAM 31

28   7 7 7   7 7 7   28

28 sts.

DIAGRAM 32

▶ *PROJECTS* ◀

► *Following the instructions for man's and woman's example sweaters, diagram and chart:*

High, round-necked slipover with opening.
High, round-necked slipover without opening.
High, round-necked cardigan.

► *Diagram and chart V-neckline for woman's example slipover sweater.*
► *Diagram and chart your own sweater to the shoulder.*
► *Check answers on pages 221 to 223.*

All sleeves should be comfortable and allow for freedom of movement. The type of sleeve depends upon the type of garment, the material used, and, of course, the needs of the individual. Any sleeve, no matter how tight-fitting, should never be skin-tight.

There are many types of sleeves: long, short, three-quarters, dolman, etc., with caps that fit into the armhole with no extra fullness, and some that are slightly gathered. Also they can be of many and varied widths according to the dictates of fashion.

In sewing today, there is only a slight difference in the right and left sleeve; whereas in knitting both the right and left sleeves are the same.

11
Sleeves

LONG SLEEVES

METHOD

1. The wrist measurement, plus one inch, times the stitch gauge provide the least number of stitches for the cuff—wider if desired.

2. Add one inch of stitches or more on the first row after the ribbing.

3. Add 2 inches or more for a woman, 3 inches for a man, and 1½ inches for a child to the upper arm measurement.

4. The difference between the stitches above the cuff or rib and the stitches required at the upper arm, equals the number of stitches to be added on both sides—½ at each.

5. Divide the number of stitches to be increased at one side into the length of sleeve above the cuff to know where to increase—allow 2 to 4 inches even.

6. For the cap, bind off the same number of stitches as the back and front underarms; then knit 2 together at the beginning and end of every other row, until 3½ inches of stitches remain; then bind off 2 stitches at the beginning of every row, until 2 inches of stitches are left. Bind off all the stitches.

Note that when sleeves are wider than the necessary increase at the upper arm, when knitting the cap, the surplus width must be reduced. Generally, at 3½ inches of stitches, we bind off 2 stitches at the beginning of the rows, but for every extra inch added, begin to bind off 2 stitches one inch sooner. For example, at 4½ inches, 5½ inches, etc.

The depth of a woman's cap is 5½ inches or more, a man's is 6½ inches or more, and a child's is 3 inches.

Half the curve around the cap should be the same as half the armhole measurement.

MEASUREMENTS

Wrist	6 inches
Upper arm	11 inches
Sleeve underarm length	18 inches

Stitch gauge—6 stitches to the inch

Follow Diagram 33.

EXAMPLE

1. 6 inches plus 1 inch at the wrist, times 6 stitches to the inch = 42 stitches. 44 stitches for K. 2, P. 2, the same as the ribbing at the bottom of the sweater. Knit 2 inches of ribbing or more. For a man, begin with 2 inches more at the wrist.

2. At least 1 inch of stitches is added on the first row after the ribbing, 6 stitches. 44 stitches plus 6 stitches = 50 stitches. 6 into 44 goes 7 times, so increase in every 7th stitch. For a man, add 2 inches or more on the first row after the ribbing.

3. The upper arm measurement is 11 inches plus 2 inches = 13 inches. 13 times 6 stitches to the inch = 78 stitches. 50 stitches from 78 stitches is 28 stitches. 14 stitches to increase on each side. (Increases should be completed from 2 to 4 inches from the underarm.) For a man, allow 3 inches more than the actual upper-arm measurement. For a child, add 1½ inches. An extra-long cuff may be knitted to add length.

4. The underarm measurement is 18 inches, so increase at both sides every inch, 14 times, then knit 2 inches even, or until underarm measures 18 inches.

5. For the cap, or top of the sleeve, bind off 6 stitches to match the underarms at the beginning of the next 2 rows; then knit 2 together at the beginning and the end of the knitted rows (front), until 3½ inches of stitches remain, 22 stitches. Now bind off 2 stitches at the beginning of every row until 2 inches of stitches are left, 12 stitches. Bind off. Around the cap of the sleeve will be the armhole measurement.

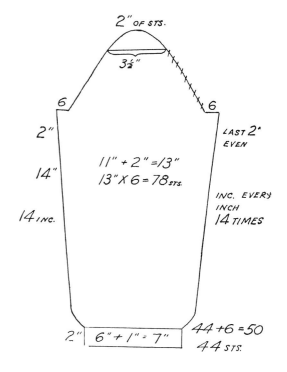

DIAGRAM 33

▶ *PROJECTS* ◀

► *Diagram and chart the man's and woman's long sleeves of the example sweaters, using 6 stitches to the* inch for the man, and 7 stitches to the inch for the woman.

► *Diagram and chart your own sweater sleeve.*
► *Check answers on pages 224 and 225.*

SHORT SLEEVES

Short sleeves may be many lengths and widths depending upon the type of material, individual needs, and the purpose of the garment. They may also be knitted with or without ribbing or bands.

A short, straight sleeve, like a long sleeve, must have at least 2 inches added to the upper arm measurement for width, and may vary from 2 inches to 5½ inches in length. The cap is finished in the same way as for a long sleeve. See Diagram 34.

A short, action sleeve is more generous in width, 3 or 4 inches more than the upper arm measurement, yet not too wide for good styling. This sleeve is characterized by the fact that it is made without a cuff. These are shaped at the underarm seam, so that too much fullness is not taken out at the seam; and the sleeve is begun with more width.

As for long sleeves, the cap should fit into the armhole; so if 3 inches of stitches are added for a woman, at the upper arm, at 4½ inches of stitches, bind off 2 stitches at the beginning of every row, until 2 inches of stitches remain, then bind off.

For a woman with large upper arms, three-quarter length sleeves are good. It may be a straight sleeve, having the necessary width at the upper arm, or may nearly fit around the forearm; and the stitches may be added immediately after the ribbing, or quickly at the sides.

To start sleeves at the bottom, work as follows:

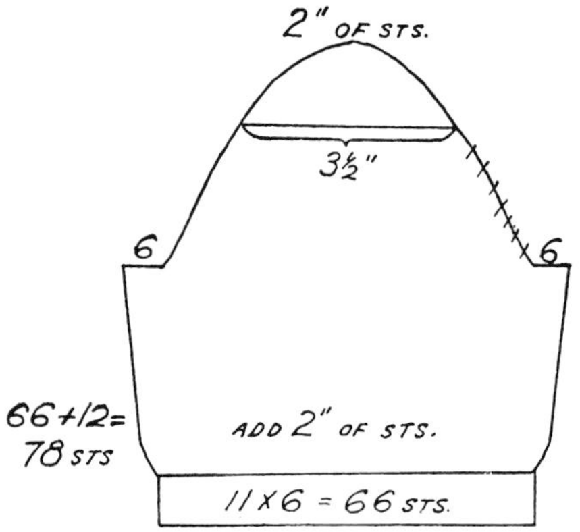

DIAGRAM 34

METHOD

➤ Use the upper arm measurement for a narrow ribbing.
➤ Add at least 2 inches of stitches on the first row after the ribbing, more if desired.
➤ Complete the cap as for the long sleeve.

To start a sleeve at the top, work as follows:

METHOD

1. Diagram and chart as though beginning at the bottom. Use the upper arm measurement for a narrow ribbing.
2. Cast on 2 inches of stitches, then add 2 stitches at the beginning of every row until you have $3\frac{1}{2}$ inches of stitches.
3. Increase a stitch at the beginning and end of every row (front) until the cap is the same size as the armhole.
4. Add the same number of stitches at each end that were bound off at the back and front underarms.
5. Continue knitting the sleeve, in reverse.

▶ *PROJECT* ◀

➤ *Diagram and chart a short sleeve, 5 inches long and 3 inches wider than the upper arm measurement for your woman's example sweater. Stitch gauge is 7 stitches to the inch.*
➤ *Check your answers on page 227.*

CAP SLEEVES

Attached caps

In this type of sleeve, no armhole is actually knitted, although it is necessary to figure the number of stitches that would be taken off at the armhole, and for the shaping of the shoulders.

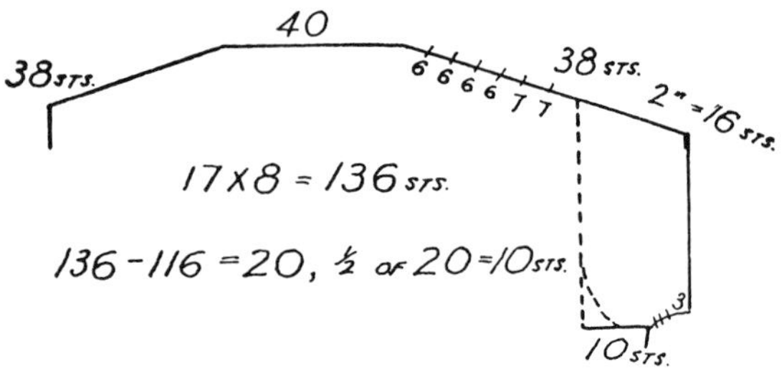

METHOD

▶ Decide the length of the cap from the shoulder, and multiply by the stitch gauge.

▶ Chart the top of the garment to find how many stitches should be taken off at the armhole.

▶ Subtract the armhole stitches from the length of the cap stitches to find how many stitches to add.

▶ Add one-half an inch of stitches, one every other row, for a slight curve at the underarm.

▶ Add the rest of the stitches at the underarm.

▶ Knit even for one-half the desired width of the cap sleeves.

MEASUREMENTS

Shoulder to shoulder—14½ inches
Across the back underarm—17 inches
Length of cap—2 inches from the tip of the shoulder
Armscye—18 inches
Stitch gauge—8 stitches to the inch.

Note that the actual cap may be 1, 2, 3 inches, or more, in length and protrude straight out from the tip of the shoulder, or it may hug the upper arm.

Follow Diagram 35 carefully.

EXAMPLE

▶ The across the back underarm measurement is 17 inches times 8 stitches to the inch = 136 stitches.

▶ The shoulder-to-shoulder measurement is 14½ inches times 8 stitches to the inch = 116 stitches.

▶ The underarm stitches, 136 minus the shoulder stitches, 116, leaves 20 stitches, that is 10 from each side.

$$40$$
$$38 srs.$$
$$6\ 6\ 6\ 7\ 7$$
$$38\ srs.$$
$$2'' = 16\ srs.$$
$$17 X 8 = 136\ srs.$$
$$136 - 116 = 20,\ \frac{1}{2}\ of\ 20 = 10\ srs.$$
$$10\ srs.$$
$$3$$

DIAGRAM 35

▶ The length of the cap is 2 inches—8 stitches to the inch = 16 stitches. That is, 16 stitches to protrude beyond the shoulder stitches.

▶ 16 stitches minus 10 stitches that were not taken off at the armscye leaves 6 stitches. See Diagram 35.

▶ Since there should be a slight curve at the armhole edge, 3 increases are made every other row, then 3 cast on at one time. We now have 16 stitches or 2 inches more than the tip of the shoulder.

Straight caps

If a straight cap from the shoulder is desired, knit even until the armscye measurement is reached, then bind off the extra 16 stitches and complete the shoulder as desired for the particular type of neckline.

Note that the actual armscye will have to be gauged when measuring. Be sure it is not too small.

Back and front low necklines are diagrammed in the same manner as previously.

Caps that hug the upper arm

If the top of the cap is to hug the upper arm, the stitches should be bound off gradually according to the closeness desired. See Diagram 36.

DIAGRAM 36

METHOD

1. Two stitches are bound off, every other row, 8 times. That takes 16 rows at 12 rows to the inch. The decreasing is started 1¼ inches before the tip of the shoulder.

2. Since the total armhole measurement is 18 inches, half is 9 inches minus 1¼ inches or 7¾ inches. That would give a sleeve width of 15½ inches. See Diagram 36.

▶ PROJECTS ◀

▶ *Using the measurements of Chapter 17, the across-the-back underarm measurement—18 inches—and the stitch gauge—7 stitches to the inch—diagram and chart.*

A 3-inch cap straight out from the shoulder.
A 3-inch cap fitting at the upper arm.

▶ *File illustrations of evening sweaters according to:*

Necklines.
Sleeves.

DOLMAN, BAT, OR WINGED SLEEVES

All these names apply to the same type of sleeve: a wider sleeve that resembles the wing of a bat.

Armhole

The only difference between the armhole of a dolman sleeve and a normal armhole is that it is deeper. For a normal set-in sleeve, we require a 17- or 18-inch armhole. A dolman sleeve has, at least, a 2-inch deeper armhole, which requires the following changes in the garment.

NORMAL SLEEVE	DOLMAN SLEEVE
Upper arm—10 inches	9 inches + 2 inches is 11 inches
Armhole—18 inches, $\frac{1}{2}$, 9 inches	$5\frac{1}{2}$ inches + 2 inches is
Cap of Sleeve—$5\frac{1}{2}$ inches deep	$7\frac{1}{2}$ inches
Underarm to waist—8 inches	8 inches − 2 inches is 6 inches
Sleeve underarm length— 18 inches	18 inches − 2 inches is 16 inches

Long dolman sleeve

This is a long dolman sleeve made at the same time as

the body of the garment with a seam at the center sleeve and shoulder.

METHOD

1. For the curve at the underarm, add 1 stitch, every other row, for 1 inch of stitches; then half an inch of stitches, every other row, until the length of the sleeve curve has been added.

2. Add the total number of stitches for the desired length of the sleeve.

3. Knit even for the desired width of the sleeve at the wrist (half the wrist measurement).

4. For sleeves of an average width, bind off half an inch of stitches, until half the length of the sleeve has been reached; then 1 inch of stitches until the shoulder line is reached. The binding off at the center seam depends upon the desired width. If no seam is desired at the center of the sleeve, reverse the shaping.

5. Bind off the shoulder stitches.

MEASUREMENTS

The underarm to waist measurement—8 inches minus 3 inches leaves 5 inches.

The underarm sleeve measurement—18 inches minus 3 inches leaves 15 inches.

Width at the wrist—8 inches, half is 4 inches.

Stitch gauge—8 stitches to the inch.

EXAMPLE

Follow Diagram 37.

1. For the curve at the underarm, add 1 stitch every other row for 1 inch, or 8 times; then add 4 stitches every other row, 4 times, making the 3-inch sleeve curve.

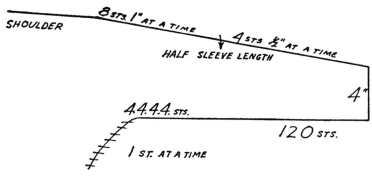

SHOULDER 8 STS. 1" AT A TIME

4 STS ½" AT A TIME

HALF SLEEVE LENGTH

4"

4.4.4.4 STS.

120 STS.

1 ST. AT A TIME

DIAGRAM 37

2. 15 inches times 8 stitches to the inch = 120 stitches, to be added all at once.

3. Knit even for 4 inches or the desired width for half the wrist measurement.

4. Bind off 4 stitches, which is half an inch of stitches, every other row, until 60 stitches have been bound off, half the length of the sleeve.

5. Bind off 1 inch of stitches until the shoulder stitches remain.

6. Bind off the shoulder stitches.

▶ PROJECTS ◀

► *State the necessary changes in measurements when using a dolman sleeve.*

► *Using the same measurements as the example, and 6 stitches to the inch, diagram and chart a long, dolman sleeve.*

► *Check the answers on page 227.*

12
Raglans

Using a circular needle we begin a knit-in raglan at the neck, working the back, sleeves, and front altogether. Continue knitting until the underarm seams are reached for sweaters and coats, and to the tips of the shoulders for capes. See Illustration 27.

A 14-inch neckline is the one chosen first because it is the size that is perfect for figuring.

The type of neckline is not considered at this point, but the number of stitches required for the increases, the back, the front, and the sleeves.

If we are going to have an opening in the front and a turned-back lapel, all the stitches are cast on at one time; but when a shaped neckline is desired, the front has to be shaped gradually in the same way as for a sweater with set-in sleeves.

MEASUREMENTS

> Neck—14 inches
> Raglan—10 inches

Stitch gauge—6 stitches to the inch
8 rows to the inch

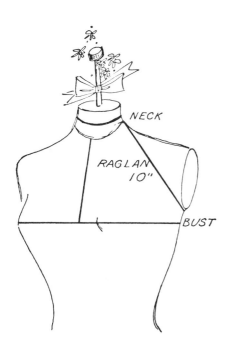

NECK

RAGLAN
10"

BUST

ILLUSTRATION 27

METHOD

► 14 inches multiplied by 6 stitches to the inch = 84 stitches for the total neckline.

► 8 stitches are needed for the increases.

► 5 inches of stitches are allowed for the back of the neck. 5 multiplied by 6 stitches to the inch is 30 stitches.

► 1 inch or 6 stitches is allotted for each sleeve; therefore 12 stitches for 2.

► We have, therefore, 8 stitches for the increases, 30 stitches for the back of the neck, 12 stitches for the sleeves, making 50 stitches. 50 stitches from the total of 84 stitches leaves 34 stitches, 17 stitches for each front.

Since it is easier to understand when all the stitches are cast on at the beginning, this method is explained first.

EXAMPLE

1. Using a circular needle, cast on 84 stitches, but do not join. Purl back, so it is easier to increase in the necessary stitches.

2. Follow Diagram 38. Knit 17 sts. for the front, increase in the next stitch, place a marker on the needle, increase in the next stitch, knit 6 sts. Sleeve, increase in the next stitch, place a marker, increase in the next stitch, knit 30 sts. Back of the neck, increase in the next stitch, place a marker, increase in the next stitch, knit 6 sts. for the other sleeve, increase in the next stitch, place a marker, increase in the next stitch, knit 17 sts. for the front.

Each of the increases made a new stitch, so there are now 84 plus 8 stitches which = 92 stitches.

3. Since there is an opening in the front, the second

row is purled (no increases), passing the markers from one needle to another.

4. For a slipover sweater, the work is joined and every second round knitted without any increases. But the number of stitches at the neckline must be increased, allowing 1 extra inch of stitches for the back of the neck, and one inch extra for the front, for a high round neck or turtle-necked sweater.

5. Continue increasing before and after the markers, every second row or round, until the raglan measures 10 inches, or the necessary bust or chest measurement has been reached.

6. Before placing the sleeve stitches on another needle, test the measurements by adding 1½ inches of sts. to the back sts. and 1½ inches to the front. Add these together and multiply by the stitch gauge to see if the chest measurement has been reached.

7. Leave all the stitches, except for one sleeve, on the circular needle. With a straight needle, add ¾ inch of sts., 4 in this case, to each side of the sleeves, as well as to the back and fronts, when we come to them.

8. Work the sleeve back and forth, reversing the shape as for a sweater with set-in sleeves.

9. Work the other sleeve.

10. Add the underarm stitches to the fronts and back —these may be worked separately or all in one.

11. Complete, in reverse, as for sweater with set-in sleeves.

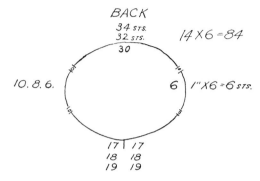

DIAGRAM 38

RAGLAN WITH OVAL NECKLINE

There were 34 stitches allotted for the front of the neck. Two of these are cast on with the stitches for the sleeves and the back of the neck, making 52 stitches, leaving 32 stitches to be added for the neck shaping, 16 stitches for each side.

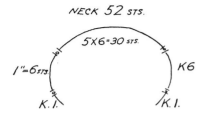

DIAGRAM 39

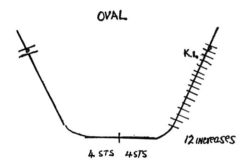

DIAGRAM 40

METHOD

► Work as previously, but increase both fronts, every other row, 1 stitch, at the neck edge, 12 times, then cast on 4 stitches each side. See Diagrams 39 and 40.

► When all the front stitches have been added, join the work and knit around and around.

▶ PROJECT ◄

► *Start sample raglans, using the same measurement and stitch gauge.*

All the stitches at one time.
With V-neckline.

As a variation, try raglans with different stitch gauges or size of necklines. For a 15-inch neckline and 6 stitches to the inch, see Diagram 41; it is self-explanatory.

For a 16-inch neckline and 7 stitches to the inch, see Diagram 42 and use the following formula.

$$16'' \times 7 = 112 \text{ sts}$$

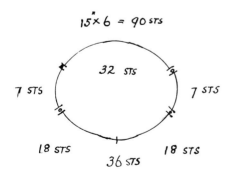

DIAGRAM 41

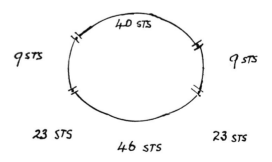

DIAGRAM 42

EXAMPLE

► 16 inches multiplied by 7 stitches to the inch is 112 stitches.

► Proportioning the stitches from the 14-inch neckline, we require 40 stitches for the back of the neck, 9 stitches for each sleeve, and 8 stitches for the increasing.

► The total is 66 sts. and 46 sts. for the total front.

For a raglan with set-in sleeves (which may be worked on a machine), diagram and chart the sweater in the same way as a sweater with set-in sleeves to the armholes, back, front, and sleeves.

METHOD

1. For the back, bind off ¾ inch of sts. on both sides, then knit 2 together at the beginning and end of every front row, until the raglan measurement is reached, and approximately 5 inches of sts. remain. See Diagram 43.

2. The front is knitted the same as the back until the neckline is reached. Using the back, count the number of stitches still to be decreased in the raglan from where the neckline is begun. See Diagram 44.

3. Subtract these from the total number of stitches to know how many to take off at the neck edge.

4. Figure the neck stitches in the same way as a sweater with set-in sleeves, and complete the raglan.

5. For the sleeves, the raglan must be the same length as the back raglan. Work the sleeve to the underarm. See Diagram 45.

6. Bind off ¾ inch of stitches on both sides.

7. Knit 2 together at the beginning and end of the front rows until the desired length of raglan is reached.

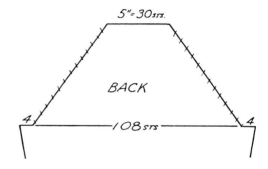

DIAGRAM 43

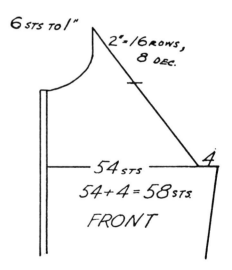

DIAGRAM 44

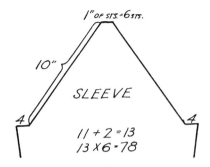

1″ OF STS. = 6 STS.

10″

SLEEVE

4   4

11 + 2 = 13
13 X 6 = 78

DIAGRAM 45

▶ **PROJECT** ◀

► *Diagram the back and left front of a raglan with set-in sleeves, with a high, round neckline, using the same measurements as in Chapter 6, and 7 sts. to the inch.*

► *See answers on page 229.*

CAPES

A well-fitting cape should lie flat across the shoulders. Increase as for raglans, until the tip of the shoulder is reached, approximately 5 to 5½ inches. The seam will show across the shoulders where the 8 increases were made. Now the 8 increases may be spread out, or, if extra fullness is desired at the back or all around, extra increases may be added, evenly distributed where the folds should fall, and the increases made on the right side of the work.

Today we consider knitting and crocheting in the same light as sewing. Each piece is shaped separately according to the necessary measurements; sleeves are made the suitable width and length; and the caps are deep enough so that neither the shoulder nor the neckline is pulled out of shape. Now the sweater has to be completed, so that we have a finished, custom-made look.

As in sewing, the ribbing at the neck, collars, etc., is completed after the larger pieces are fastened together, with the exception of a slipover sweater without an opening—the ribbing at the front is knitted first.

The seams used to be either woven or overcast together on the wrong side, which is all right for baby sweaters and very fine yarn; but a much better way is to slip stitch (crochet) the pieces together on the wrong side. A #5 steel crochet hook is adequate for nearly all types of materials. Never use a bone hook, because it makes the stitches too loose. See Chapter 4.

13

Finishing and Blocking Sweaters

SLIP STITCH IN CROCHET

METHOD

1. Place the two seams together, wrong side out, and insert the hook through the two folds not quite one-eighth of an inch deep.

2. Place the thread over the hook and draw the thread through the folds and the loop on the hook. Split the yarn if it is too heavy. Be sure the seams are as elastic as the rest of the garment; but they should not show on the right side.

3. Join the underarm seams, sleeve seams, then shoulders. When putting the shoulders together, slip-stitch deeper at the beginning of each slope.

4. Pin in the sleeves at the armholes, with the seam at the underarm seam, and the center of the top of the cap at the shoulder seam. Slip-stitch in place.

PICKING UP STITCHES AROUND THE NECK

Become accustomed to using your tapemeasure. For slip-over, round necklines, measure from the shoulder seam to the center front. If this is 5½ inches; and there are 6 stitches to the inch, use an even number of stitches for each side—68 stitches from shoulder to shoulder seam. For the back of the neck, the same number of stitches are used as were bound off.

Pick up the stitches around a neckline or armhole for ribbing, or the completion of a pocket, on the right side. For collars, measure the length as above, but pick up the stitches on the wrong side.

If smaller needles are used for picking up the stitches

around a neckline, the gauge of the smaller needles must be used.

METHOD

► Place the point of the needle into a stitch.
► Pass the yarn around the needle as if to knit and draw the loop through to make a stitch. Be sure to put the needle in deep enough so that no holes are formed. Picked up stitches should look like a continuation of the fabric.

Picking up stitches near knit-2-together decreases can sometimes be a problem. It is better not to pick up the loose stitch between the two decreases (for this causes a hole) rather to pick up a stitch immediately below the actual decrease, then one in the decrease itself.

Knit the knits and *purl the purls* when binding off. The ribbing is generally one-inch wide, or six to eight inches for a turtleneck.

MITER FOR A V-NECK

METHOD

► Mark the center of the V with a safety pin.
► Measure the inches, thus the stitches to the center front, as for a round neckline.
► Allow 2 knit stitches right in the center of the V and 4 purl stitches on each side. This is done by counting from the center after all the stitches have been picked up; so, coming back on the wrong side, it will be K. 4, P. 2, K. 4, in the center.
► Decrease on the 4 purl stitches, on both sides of the K. 2, every front row, until P. 1 remains. If necessary, K. 2 together in the center.

RIBBON DOWN THE FRONT

If ribbon is going to be sewn down the front, it is better to do this after the sweater has been steamed. Then the correct length of the ribbon can be ascertained. I suggest measuring the length when the sweater is worn. Allow one extra inch of ribbon for turn-unders.

METHOD

1. Baste and overcast the ribbon.
2. Baste the buttonholes and the ribbon together.
3. Cut the buttonholes in the ribbon.
4. Buttonhole stitch on both the sweater and the ribbon at the same time.

COLLARS

Round, flat collar for a high, round neckline

METHOD

1. Measure the inches from the center front to the shoulder seam and multiply by the stitch gauge.
2. Pick up the stitches, on the wrong side, from the center front to the shoulder seam. Continue around the back, picking up the same number of stitches as were bound off, then pick up the stitches on the other half front.
3. Purl a row, knit a row, purl a row, and on the 4th row, increase before and after the shoulder seams. This makes 4 increases.
4. Continue to increase every 4th row, about one inch

from each shoulder seam, until the desired depth of collar.

5. Single crochet twice around the collar to make it lie flat.

Stand-up collar

For a collar that stands up at the back, use the following method.

METHOD

1. Pick up the stitches in the same way as for a round collar.

2. Knit even in stockinette stitch or ribbing, as desired, for 3½ or 4 inches.

3. If points are desired at the front, increase at the beginning and end of every 4th row. (If stockinette stitch is used, single crochet on the right side twice, tightly.)

Lapels

The simplest lapels to make are those on which the neckline is not bound off (see the illustration) and the garment is knitted straight at the center front. The shoulders are shaped when the armhole measurement is reached; then the remaining stitches are bound off loosely. This, of course, gives the wrong side of the material when the lapel is turned to the front; but if the remainder of the stitches for the collar are knitted on the wrong side, this is permissible.

Decrease the same as for a V-neckline and knit separate pieces for lapels, starting with 4 stitches and increasing where you decreased on the garment. If a wider lapel is desired, increase at the outer edge. The dart stitches in a jacket may be used to widen a lapel.

ILLUSTRATION 28

Notched collar

METHOD

1. Pick up the stitches on the right side of the lapel (about 2 inches from the shoulder seam, depending upon the width) around the back of the neck, then the other lapel.
2. Work for 3½ inches.
3. Bind off loosely and crochet around the lapels and collar, twice on the right side to make them stay flat.

Rolled collars

METHOD

1. Pick up all the stitches at one time, on the wrong side (see round collar).
2. Work 6 rows even, then bind off half an inch of stitches at the beginning of every row, until the desired width of the collar.
3. Bind off all the stitches loosely.
4. Single crochet twice to keep the collar flat.

▶ *PROJECT* ◀

➤ *Make a small V-neckline and miter the V.*
➤ *Complete your own sweater.*

BLOCKING

Actually, a sweater knitted from correct measurements should not have to be blocked. It should just be steamed flat. A steam iron is excellent for this. Have you tried the sweater on to see how the shoulders fit? Did you tighten the armscye when putting in the sleeve? Are all your seams elastic? Does it feel comfortable? Are your stitches picked up neatly? Are you satisfied with the result? Can you diagram and chart any type of slipover or cardigan (not fitted) using any material and for any person? You should be able to, since that has been the purpose of the previous chapters. From now on, we shall apply the techniques of shaping to other garments.

In the first place, I definitely do not agree with blocking any garment made of wool, or partly-wool yarn, in separate pieces. The elasticity of the yarn allows the pieces to be stretched; and I have seen some sad shapes, when supposedly blocked in pieces, by someone who did not understand what she was doing.

Ribbon knits are a different matter, as has been discussed in Chapter 5.

Materials for blocking

▶ A large table.
▶ A heavy pad for a base to which the garment may be pinned.
▶ Cloth to cover the pad—unbleached muslin is satisfactory.
▶ A long wooden rule.
▶ Non-rusting blocking pins.
▶ Steam or electric iron.
▶ Cloths for steaming, which should be neither too thick nor too thin. Used Turkish towels are good.
▶ A sleeve-pressing board.

METHOD

1. Turn the sweater inside out. (Follow Diagram 46.)
2. With pins, mark the center back of the sweater.
3. On the blocking board place pins at "A" and "B,"

where the center back is to be pinned. Pin the center back to the board.

4. With the rule, mark a line "CD," where the waist is pinned, using half the waist measurement, one-quarter on each side of "AB." Note that the center back and sides are pinned before the fronts are pinned down in a cardigan.

5. At "D," measure "DF," which is the underarm to waist measurement.

6. Measure "EF" which is half the bust measurement, one-quarter on each side of "AB."

7. Pin the sweater to measurements and check.

8. Spread the armscyes until the correct measurement is obtained. Pin to the board.

9. Test the shoulders to see if they are the correct width—adjust the width by means of the armscyes; then pin to the board, being sure that both sides are equidistant from the center.

10. If the sweater is a cardigan, pin down the center fronts, allowing for overlap.

11. Adjust the neckline and pin in position.

12. Measure the sleeve underarm length and pin the sleeves in position, "EK" and "FJ."

13. Check the width of the sleeves and pin.

14. Dampen a cloth in warm water and place it over the garment.

15. Steam with a hot iron, but be sure to keep the weight of iron in the *hand*. If the weight is allowed to press down the wool, it will leave a shiny mark and shrink it. (Never steam ribbing, since it should not be stretched.) A steam iron may be used instead of cloth if there is definitely no stretching required.

16. Leave the sweater on the pad until it is dry.

17. Take out the pins; steam the seams using the sleeve board where necessary. Be sure to remove the pin marks. If the garment is made to fit, place the pins one inch apart—more may be needed if it is tight.

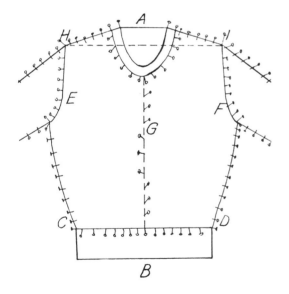

DIAGRAM 46

Generally speaking, sleeveless sweaters are badly de-signed in knitting. I have seen celebrities in advertise-ments wearing sleeveless sweaters that were very poorly styled, having tight armholes and shoulders that were too long. To allow for freedom of movement, there should be no constriction at the armhole or the neckline.

There are 5 main differences between diagramming and charting a sleeveless sweater from doing one with set-in sleeves.

► The underarm to waist measurement is one inch shorter.

► Half the armhole measurement is one inch longer, to make up for the one inch deducted from the underarm-to-waist measurement.

► The shoulder-to-shoulder measurement is one inch shorter on each side, which means two inches altogether.

► The one inch deducted from the shoulders is added to the first bind-off, at the armhole.

► Allow one fewer slope at the shoulders according to the stitch gauge.

14
Sleeveless Garments

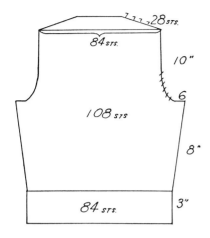

DIAGRAM 47

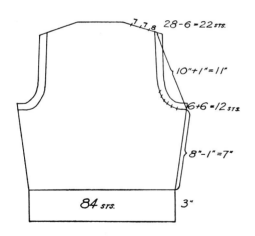

DIAGRAM 48

See Diagrams 47 and 48, using measurements from Chapter 6. They are self-explanatory.

Remember to always diagram and chart the body of a sweater with set-in sleeves first.

The stitches around the armhole are picked up after the body of the sweater is completed. This is one inch wide, making the full shoulder-to-shoulder measurement.

The neckline is finished the same as for a sweater with set-in sleeves.

CABLES

Turn to Chapter 18 for the rule concerning cables.

EXAMPLE

1. 2 extra stitches are added for each cable, which means that 10 extra stitches must be added for 5 cables, etc.

2. Using figures from Diagram 47, and adding 5 cables to the body of the sweater of P. 2, K. 6, P. 2, that is, 108 stitches plus 10 stitches, which makes 118 stitches.

3. Each cable requires 10 stitches, so 5 cables equal 5 times 10, which is 50 stitches.

4. 50 stitches from 118 stitches leaves 68 stitches for 6 spaces.

5. 6 into 68 goes 11 times and 2 over, so knit 11 stitches between each cable, except at the ends where you have to knit 12 stitches. See Diagram 49.

Always diagram without the cables first, then add the extra stitches for the body of the sweater. Thus, the figuring will be the same as for a sweater without cables, except for the figuring of the first cable row.

For the shaping at the armhole, neck, and shoulders,

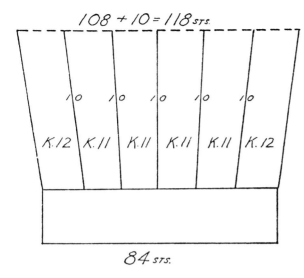

108 + 10 = 118 STS.

K.12   K.11   K.11   K.11   K.11   K.12

84 STS.

DIAGRAM 49

knit 2 together twice at each cable to eliminate the extra stitches.

It is not necessary to have cables both at the back and front of a sweater: Cables are often placed at the front, with one or two for the sleeves.

▶ PROJECT ◀

▶ *On the sample measurements of Chapter 6 on page 45, diagram and chart the backs of sleeveless sweaters for both a man and woman.*

▶ *On the man's measurements of Chapter 6, diagram the front of a cable sweater to the armhole, having 5 cables of P. 2, K. 6, P. 2 evenly spaced.*

▶ *Check answers on pages 227 through 229.*

Fitted weskits and jerkins are diagrammed and charted in the same way as sleeveless sweaters, except for the increases for the bust, which are gradually added at the sides.

METHOD

1. Half the waist measurement subtracted from half the bust measurement equals the number of stitches to add at the underarm seams.

2. Divide by 2 to find the number of stitches to add at each side.

3. Divide the number of stitches to increase into the inches at the underarm seam, to know where to increase.

(Since the fullest part of the bust comes from 2 to 4 inches below the armpit, it is better to complete all the increases before that point.)

15

Fitted Weskits and Jerkins

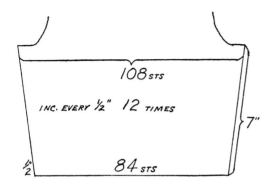

DIAGRAM 50

For the example, the same measurements will be used as those given in Chapter 6.

1. For a weskit, the 84 stitches for the waist (back) are subtracted from across the 108 back underarm stitches, which leaves 24 stitches. See Diagram 50.

2. There are 7 inches to the underarm; therefore, if one stitch is increased on both sides, every ½ inch, 12 times, and the last 1 inch is knitted even, there will be 108 stitches.

BANDS AND POCKETS

Although weskits and jerkins do not have actual bands down the front, extra stitches must be allowed, just as for a cardigan, and the position of the buttons must be marked first.

Since a weskit is a tight-fitting garment, many buttonholes are required; one inch to one-and-a-half inches apart is satisfactory. Be sure the top buttonhole is in the correct position before starting any of the buttonholes.

The position of the pockets is exactly the same for weskits as for any other garment.

FRONTS

EXAMPLE

► Charting the left front without any points and allowing 4 extra stitches on both sides for buttons and buttonholes, there would be half of the 84 stitches, 42 stitches plus 4 stitches = 46 stitches at the waist.

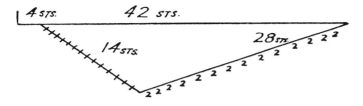

DIAGRAM 51

► Increase at the underarm seam, the same as the back, making the last inch even.

Points at the front

The points come toward the center front, allowing one-third of the number of stitches and two-thirds toward the underarm seam. They are from three to three-and-a-half inches in depth, with the greatest slope toward the front.

EXAMPLE

1. One-third of 42 stitches is 14 stitches, and two-thirds is 28 stitches.

2. Start the left front first with 2 stitches and increase 1 stitch toward the center front and 2 toward the underarm seam, every other row, until 42 stitches are made.

3. Add the last 4 stitches all at one time for the overlap at the front, making 46 stitches, the desired number. See Diagram 51.

► PROJECT ◄

► *Diagram and chart a weskit left front, with a square neckline on the woman's sample measurements in Chapter 6.*

► *Check the answer on pages 229 and 230.*

16
Fitted Sweaters

It is well to remember that only a person with a good figure and perfect carriage should wear tight-fitting garments; this applies especially to fitted sweaters, and even then, one must always allow sufficient room for freedom of movement. With the advent of scientifically designed girdles and bras, more women have reasonably good figures than previously.

Do not have a false impression about knits, however. Remember, I said "tight-fitting garments." Any woman may wear knits, if they are correctly styled. That is why, throughout the entire course, I have stressed the correct method of measurements and individual design.

In the previous chapter we considered weskits fitted at the underarm seam.

One more measurement is required for a fitted sweater than for a weskit, if it starts below the waist. Again, we must be careful that the length suit individual needs.

At the desired depth, take the measurement around the body. Care must be taken that the tape does not drop either at the front or back, and it must be loose enough so the flat of the hand may pass under the tape.

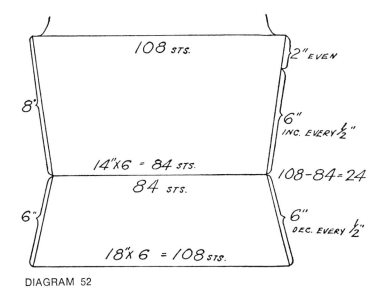

DIAGRAM 52

► Use the same method as that applied to fitted sweaters.

► But use the underarm to waist and armhole measurements that were used for a sweater with set-in sleeves. See Diagram 52.

MEASUREMENTS

Waist	28 inches
Bust	36 inches
Waist to underarm	8 inches
Armhole	18 inches
Hip (6 inches below the waist)	36 inches

Stitch gauge—6 stitches to the inch.

Study Diagram 52. It is self-explanatory.

You will notice that, generally, the fronts and backs of tight-fitting sweaters are the same width. For sweaters for the evening it may be necessary to allow more width at the front. This will be discussed in Chapter 17.

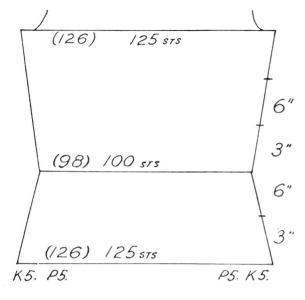

DIAGRAM 53

RIBBED FITTED SWEATERS

Ribbed fitted sweaters are decreased and increased in the same manner. If the ribs are large, however, and there are too many increases and decreases to be made at the sides, it is advisable to have the increases and decreases in the ribs at even intervals. See Diagram 53.

It should be understood that both sides of a ribbed garment should be the same, so that if we begin with K. 5 of a K. 5, P. 5 rib, we should end with K. 5; therefore, the number should be divisible by 10 plus 5.

The same measurements given previously are used.

EXAMPLE

▶ There are 25 stitches to decrease to the waist in 13 knitted ribs and 12 purled ribs.

► Knit 3 inches even, then decrease in the knit ribs, 13 stitches, and 3 more inches and decrease in the purl ribs, 12 stitches.

► Increase in a similar manner, ending with 2 inches even.

▶ PROJECT ◀

► *Using the measurements and stitch gauge of the woman's sweater in Chapter 6 and considering the measurement around the hip 36 inches, 6 inches below the waist, diagram the front of a fitted sweater with oval neckline, starting 4 inches below the tip of the shoulder.*

► *Check answers on page 230.*

17
Evening Sweaters

Sheer glamor for evening! Evening sweaters are sophisticated for after dark in America—bare-shouldered, scoop necklines, with or without slender, tapering sleeves, cap sleeves, or no sleeves, made of very fine wool or linen yarn intermingled with metallic thread and contrasted with short or full-length skirts.

If you have understood the instructions so far, it should not be difficult to transform the knowledge, with added suggestions, to evening sweaters.

NECKLINES

First we shall consider lower necklines.

As we learned in our earlier lessons on necklines (Chapter 10), they are extremely important in dress design. Strange as it may seem, low necklines are flattering for older women, especially those who take care of their carriage and have no "dowager's hump." The wrinkles around the throat line may be concealed by

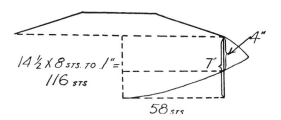

$14\frac{1}{2} \times 8$ STS. TO $1"=$
116 STS

7"

4"

58 STS

DIAGRAM 54

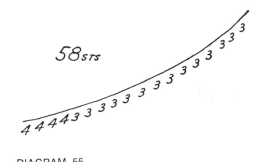

58 STS

4 4 4 4 3 3 3 3 3 3 3 3 3 3 3 3

DIAGRAM 55

means of ropes of beads, ribbon with flowers spilling from the throat, or a small knitted scarf, etc.

Having decided the type of neckline for both the front and back, with tapemeasure held horizontally across from armhole to armhole, the depth of the center front of the neckline-to-be, measure the distance from the tip of the shoulder. Also measure the depth of the neckline at the armhole.

Follow Diagrams 54 and 55. This is advanced work and will require some study.

Wide, off-shoulder, curved neckline

METHOD

1. Knit to the center.
2. According to the stitch gauge, find the number of rows in the curve at the neck edge; then divide by 2 to learn the number of rows on which to decrease.
3. Divide the number of rows into the number of stitches to ascertain how many are to be bound off at one time.
4. Add any extra stitches, one stitch at a time, to the first decreases.
5. Knit the other half to correspond, only in reverse.

MEASUREMENTS

Shoulder to shoulder—14½ inches
Center of Neckline—7 inches below the tip of
the shoulder and 4 inches down.
Stitch Gauge—8 stitches to the inch
12 rows to the inch

EXAMPLE

► Since the neckline begins 7 inches from the tip of the shoulder and ends 4 inches from the tip of the shoulder, there are 3 inches in which to take off 58 stitches gradually.

► 12 rows to the inch times 3 inches = 36 rows; but we can only bind off every other row, so there are 18 rows in which to decrease.

► 18 into 58 goes 3 times and 4 over; that means there are 4 rows at the beginning, where 4 stitches are bound off and 14 rows of 3's.

For a sleeve ending at the neck edge, the cap of the sleeve is only partially completed. Decrease the cap, as in Chapter 11, until it fits into the reduced armhole, 4 inches less than half the total armhole measurement.

Neckline for a sleeveless sweater

METHOD

► Measure the distance around the upper arm where the neckline ends.

► According to the width of the band desired, knit a piece *stretching* it to the desired length, so the strap will keep in position.

► When the sweater is completed, sew the straps in place and single-crochet tightly around the neck edge and the straps, on the right side, or, if necessary, catch-stitch narrow elastic inside the neck edge and bands.

▶ *PROJECT* ◀

► *Diagram and chart a wide, off-shoulder neckline.*

Measurements—Shoulder to shoulder—15 inches
Stitch Gauge— 7 stitches to the inch
10 rows to the inch

► *The neckline to start 6 inches down and 2 inches below the tip of the shoulder.*

ILLUSTRATION 29

▶ This requires a little concentration—you can do it!
▶ Check your answer on pages 231 and 232.

Wide, on-shoulder oval neckline

METHOD

1. Diagram and chart the shoulders.
2. Knit to the center and subtract the stitches to be used at the shoulder to ascertain how many stitches are to be decreased at the neckline.
3. According to the stitch gauge, find the number of rows on which to decrease.
4. Subtract the number of rows from the number of stitches to learn the number of stitches to bind off at the center.
5. Knit 2 together, every front row, at the neck edge, until the shoulder stitches remain.
6. Bind off the shoulder stitches.
7. Knit the other side to correspond.
8. Check the armhole measurement and, if necessary, knit even until the correct length.

MEASUREMENTS

Shoulder-to-shoulder—14½ inches
Stitch gauge— 8 stitches to the inch
12 rows to the inch

Neckline to start 6 inches below the tip of the shoulder, using 2 shoulder slopes. If any part of the shoulder line is to be used, the shoulders must be diagrammed and charted.

EXAMPLE

▶ 14½ inches times 8 stitches to the inch = 116 stitches.

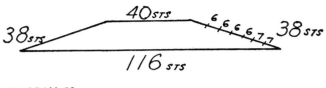

DIAGRAM 56

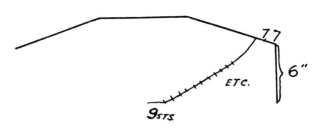

DIAGRAM 57

► 8 stitches to the inch; therefore there are 6 slopes at the shoulder. See Diagrams 56 and 57.

► Knit halfway across the 116 stitches (58 stitches). Place the remaining 58 stitches on a stitch holder.

► There are 12 rows to the inch; therefore 6 times 12 are 72 rows. Binding off every other row means 36 rows on which to decrease.

► Since 14 stitches remain at the shoulder, 58 minus 14 stitches leaves 44 stitches to decrease in 36 rows. 44 stitches minus 35 rows—one of the 36 rows for the first bind-off—gives us 9 stitches and the rest decreased by knitting 2 together, every front row, at the neck edge, and finally the two, sevens at the shoulder.

► The other side is completed similarly, only in reverse.

A wide, square, on-shoulder neckline

METHOD

1. Bind off the center stitches.
2. Knit the left side to the shoulder.
3. Shape the shoulder.
4. Knit the right side to correspond, only in reverse.

As for any type of neckline, measure the depth from the tip of the shoulder.

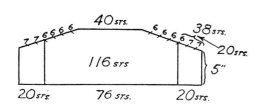

DIAGRAM 58

MEASUREMENTS

Shoulder-to-shoulder—14½ inches
Stitch Gauge— 8 stitches to the inch
12 rows to the inch

The neckline starts 5 inches below the tip of the shoulder and uses 3 shoulder slopes. See Diagram 58.

EXAMPLE

1. 14½ times 8 stitches to the inch is 116 stitches.
2. 8 stitches to the inch; therefore, there are 6 steps for each shoulder. Using 3 slopes, there are 20 stitches, 40 for both shoulders.
3. 40 stitches from 116 leaves 76 stiches to bind off for the neckline.
4. Knit 20 stitches. Bind off 76 stitches.
5. Knit even on the 20 stitches until the armhole measurement is reached; then shape the shoulder.
6. Work the other side to correspond, only in reverse.

▸ *PROJECTS* ◂

▸ *Diagram and chart a wide, on-shoulder, oval neckline using the same measurements and stitch gauge as the project in Chapter 17, the neckline to start 5 inches below the tip of the shoulder and using 2 shoulder slopes.*
▸ *Diagram and chart a wide, square, on-shoulder neckline, using the same measurements and stitch gauge as Project 1, the neckline to start 6 inches below the tip of the shoulder and using 3 slopes.*
▸ *Check the answers on pages 231 to 232.*

18
Texture Stitches

Are you going to use a different stitch for your sweater in the front? I mean a texture stitch, not a lace pattern. What are texture stitches? The texture of cloth means the surface quality or the way it looks on top, or, in knitting, the way the knits and purls are placed. Some of the texture stitches have no influence upon the apparent size of a person, while others possess a slimming effect: diagonal patterns, for example. Some make a person look larger. Cable stitches, with their bulk, have a tendency to increase breadth; but if they are used sparingly, in the form of up and down stripes, they add length.

HAND STITCHES

Pebble rib

For a multiple of two stitches, work in the following manner. See Illustration 30:

Row 1: * K. 1, P. 1, repeat from * across the row.
Row 2: Purl.

ILLUSTRATION 30

ILLUSTRATION 31

ILLUSTRATION 32

ILLUSTRATION 33

The next pattern has a multiple of 6 stitches plus 3 stitches. That means that each pattern requires 6 stitches; so, if 3 patterns were used, 18 stitches would be necessary, plus 3 stitches for the beginning and end of the row—21 stitches altogether. See Illustration 31.

Row 1: K. 1, * P. 1, K. 5, repeat from * ending P. 1, K. 1.
Row 2: K. 1, * P. 1, K. 1, P. 3, K. 1, repeat from * ending P. 1, K. 1.
Row 3: K. 1, * K. 2, P. 1, K. 1, P. 1, K. 1, repeat from * ending K. 2.
Row 4: K. 1, * P. 3, K. 1, P. 2, repeat from * ending P. 1, K. 1.
Repeat the 4 rows for pattern.

For a multiple of 7 stitches plus five, work in the following manner: See Illustration 32.

Row 1: Knit.
Row 2: Purl.
Row 3: K. 1, * K. 3, P. 4, repeat from * ending K. 4.
Row 4: K. 1, * P. 3, K. 4, repeat from * ending P. 3, K. 1.
Repeat the 4 rows.

For a multiple of 4 stitches plus 3, work as follows:

Row 1: K. 1, * K. 1, P. 3, repeat from * ending K. 2.
Row 2: K. 1, * P. 2, K. 2, repeat from * ending P. 1, K. 1.
Row 3: K. 1, * K. 1, P. 1, K. 2, repeat from * ending K. 2.
Row 4: Purl.
Repeat the 4 rows. See Illustration 33.

For a multiple of 6 stitches plus 2, work as follows:

Rows 1 and 5: * P. 2, K. 4, repeat from * ending P. 2.
Rows 2 and 4: * K. 2, P. 4, repeat from * ending K. 2.

Rows 5 and 7: * P. 3, K. 2, P. 1, repeat from * ending P. 2.

Rows 6 and 8: * K. 3, P. 2, K. 1, repeat from * ending K. 2.

Row 9: Purl.

Row 10: Knit.

Repeat 10 rows for pattern. See Illustration 34.

Cable

For a multiple of 8 stitches plus 6, work as follows:

Row 1: K. 1, * K. 4, P. 4, repeat from * ending K. 5.

Row 2: P. 1, * P. 4, K. 4, repeat from * ending P. 5.

Rows 3 and 4: Repeat rows 1 and 2.

Row 5: K. 1. * With double pointed needle slip the next 2 stitches on to it, from the back, knit the next 2 stitches, then knit 2 stitches on the double pointed needle, P. 4, * ending K. 5.

Row 6: Same as Row 2.

Repeat the 6 rows. See Illustration 35.

Extra stitches have to be allowed for cables as they tighten the work. 2 extra stitches are necessary for each. That means that if 5 cables are used, 10 extra stitches should be added on the first row after the ribbing, as well as the necessary stitches for the bust. The diagramming, however, is the same as without the cables, reducing 2 stitches at every cable when a change of shaping is made.

ILLUSTRATION 34

ILLUSTRATION 35

MACHINE STITCHES

Different tension

A number of rows are knitted with a loose stitch or different tension. See Illustration 36.

ILLUSTRATION 36

ILLUSTRATION 37

Work 13 rows with the tension set at 4.
Work 8 rows with the tension set at 10.

Skipped stitches

The needles are put out of service at certain distances from each other. See Illustration 37.

> Put every second needle out of service.
> Knit in the usual way.

Note that some machines will not take thick yarn using every needle; then every second stitch is used.

Resting position

> Work 3 rows.
> Raise every 3rd needle into resting position.
> Work 4 rows.
> Bring resting needles back into working position.
> Repeat the 4 steps.
> See Illustration 38.

Crossed stitches

Two consecutive stitches are crossed at regular intervals.

> Knit 6 rows.
> By means of tools, cross stitches 13 and 14, 19 and 20, 25 and 26, always leaving 4 knit stitches between.
> Repeat the first 2 steps, alternating pattern as in Illustration 39.

Cables

There may be 4, 6, or 8 stitches in each cable. Change the position of half the stitches, so that the first half is knitted last, and vice versa.

For example, if there are 4 stitches for the cable, hook the cable tools on the first 2 and last 2 needles, keeping the tools parallel to the needles. Cross them, then replace the stitches on the needles beneath the open latch.

See Hand Cables on page 115.

ILLUSTRATION 38

BUTTONHOLES

By hand

The most important buttonhole is the neck buttonhole. If ribbing is going to be used at the neck edge, this should be 1 inch deep and the buttonhole placed in the center. If a cardigan is fitted at the waist and the ribbing is 3 inches wide, work 2 buttonholes in the ribbing, 1 inch apart, and the rest 2 to 2½ inches.

METHOD

1. Bind off the necessary number of stitches on the right side, and knit across the row.
2. On the wrong side, purl to where the stitches are bound off—this is where many have difficulty.
3. Turn the work to add the stitches that are knitted on.
4. Knit into the stitch on the left-hand needle; don't take off the loop, but turn the stitch just made and place it on the left hand needle.
5. Add the same number of stitches that were bound off. Turn the work again and purl to the end.
6. Finish each buttonhole with buttonhole stitch after the garment has been completed.

ILLUSTRATION 39

By machine

FIRST METHOD

1. Using separate piece of yarn, lay a contrasting

piece of yarn in the heads of the needles where the buttonhole is going to be made.

2. Push the needles back to working position and continue knitting back and forth.

3. When work is completed, pull out the separate length of yarn, leaving unlocked stitches.

4. Stitch around by hand and finish with buttonhole stitch.

SECOND METHOD

1. This is somewhat like a hand-knitted buttonhole. Rest all needles except those that come ahead of the buttonhole.

2. Knit to the buttonhole and rest the stitches just made.

3. Bind off the stitches for the buttonhole, ending with 2 stitches on one needle.

4. Place all the needles in working position and knit one row.

5. Work back to the buttonhole and cast on the same number of stitches that were bound off.

6. Work the rest of the row.

▶ *PROJECT* ◀

► *Knit samples of cables and buttonholes.*

In all garments, the type of stitch that should be used is very important. A lace stitch for a tight-fitting garment is taboo. The beauty of lace, no matter how a garment is designed, lies in its delicate beauty and soft folds. The portion below the waist on a sweater or blouse, however, may be fitted and knitted in stockinette stitch, then the increasing for the lace added at the waist, just as for basic sweaters. Take the stitch gauge from a sample of the lace stitch which has been steamed, but not stretched.

Be sure you know the lace pattern before starting any garment. You will save hours of time and discouragement. This type of work entails a great deal of very careful knitting. Lace garments are exquisite for tea, cocktails, or evening occasions. If one has a knit shop or gives instructions, however, it is advisable to steer clear of intricate lace patterns: First, it is from the sale of materials that one's livelihood depends; and fine yarn, where little weight is used, means less material. Second, shaping with lace patterns is often difficult for the layman.

19
Lace Stitches

NECKLINES

When using lace patterns, it is advisable to have a stockinette stitch yoke; then no difficulty is encountered when shaping. If, however, lace is desired right up to the neckline, a square one is the simplest; so use this type if possible. If a round neckline is desired, follow the same directions as those given for the armhole shaping, which follow:

Allow one or more whole patterns for the shaping. For example, if there are 12 whole patterns for across the back, and there are 8 whole patterns for the shoulder, that means that 2 patterns are to be taken off for each armhole. After binding off one whole pattern, place a marker after the second pattern, and keep these stitches using stockinette stitch until all the stitches have been decreased.

PATTERNS FOR HAND KNITTING

First pattern

For a multiple of 6 stitches plus 1, work as follows (YO means Yarn Over):

Row 1: * K. 1, K. 2 together, YO, K. 1, YO, K. 2 together, repeat from * ending K. 1.
Row 2: Purl.
Rows 3 to 6: Repeat Rows 1 and 2, twice.
Row 7: Knit.
Row 8: Purl.
Repeat the 8 rows.

Alternate the pattern by starting with K. 3; then continue as above.

Second pattern

For a multiple of 8 stitches plus 1, work as follows:

Row 1: K. 3, * YO, Slip 1, K. 2 together, pass slip stitch over K, YO, K. 5, repeat from * across the row, ending YO, Slip 1, K. 2 together, pass, YO, K. 3.
Row 2 and all even rows: Purl.
Row 3: K. 2 together, K. 1, * YO, K. 3, YO, K. 1, Slip 1, K. 2 together, pass, K. 1, repeat from * across, ending YO, K. 3, YO, K. 1, K. 2 together.
Row 5: K. 2 together, * YO, K. 5, YO, Slip 1, K. 2 together, pass, repeat from * across, ending YO, K. 5, YO, K. 2 together.
Row 7: K. 2, * YO, K. 1, Slip 1, K. 2 together, pass, K. 1, YO, K. 3, repeat from * across, ending K. 2 instead of K. 3.
Row 8: Purl.
Repeat rows 1 to 8.

ILLUSTRATION 40

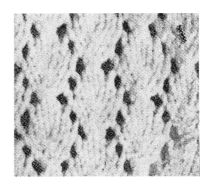

ILLUSTRATION 41

PATTERNS FOR MACHINE

Since lace patterns require much moving of stitches on a machine, always try to use a simple pattern that will look well with the least amount of changing the position of stitches.

In machine-knitting, as in hand-knitting, yarn-overs are the basis for all lace patterns along with knit-2-togethers to make up for the extra stitch that was added.

Two stitches are placed on one needle, either to the right or left, and the empty needle left in working position to take the place of the yarn-over. Then, on the next row, all the stitches are worked, creating a hole. Bearing this in mind, a lace pattern intended for hand-knitting may be worked on a machine. See Illustration 40.

First pattern

1. Transfer stitches 4, 10, 16, etc., onto needles 3, 9, 15, etc., stitches 6, 12, 18 onto needles 7, 13, 19 (the same as knit 2 together).

2. Keep the empty needles in working position and knit across twice.

3. Repeat steps 1 and 2 twice more.

4. Knit 5 rows; then alternate the pattern, as in Illustration 41.

Second pattern

1. Transfer every 8th stitch to the next needle at the left.

2. Knit across twice.

3. Counting from the left, transfer stitches 9, 17, 25, etc., to their adjacent needles at the right, and 7, 15, 23, etc., to their next needles at the left.

4. Knit across twice.

5. Transfer stitches 10, 18, 26, etc., to their next needles at the right, and stitches 6, 14, 22, etc., to their next needles at the left.

6. Knit across twice.

7. Transfer stitches 11, 19, 27, etc., to their adjacent needles at the right, and stitches 5, 13, 21, etc., to their adjacent needles to the left.

8. Knit across twice.

9. Repeat steps 1 through 8, alternating the pattern as in Illustration 42.

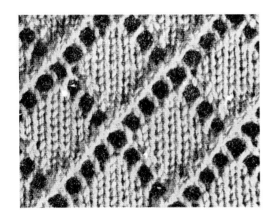

ILLUSTRATION 42

SIMULTANEOUS KNITTING AND WEAVING

Whether one considers patterns of two or more colors of Scottish origin, Fair Isle, so named, or one of the Swedish Homesloyds, does not make much difference. It should be stated, however, that each province of Sweden has its own particular pattern, and if a woman from the north visits the south, it is possible to tell from which province she came, by merely looking at her mittens.

Many knitters have difficulty with this type of knitting: changing and attaching the different colored threads, as well as having long, unsightly loops at the back of the work. This is not necessary, if one learns to *knit* and *weave* at the same time.

Before starting any two-colored design, learn how to carry and fasten the strands. There should never be long loose loops at the back of the work. It is possible for the colors to be woven in. Naturally, this takes a little practice, especially on the back, or purl, side (if not making mittens or hats, for which one uses a set of needles and

20

Changing Colors

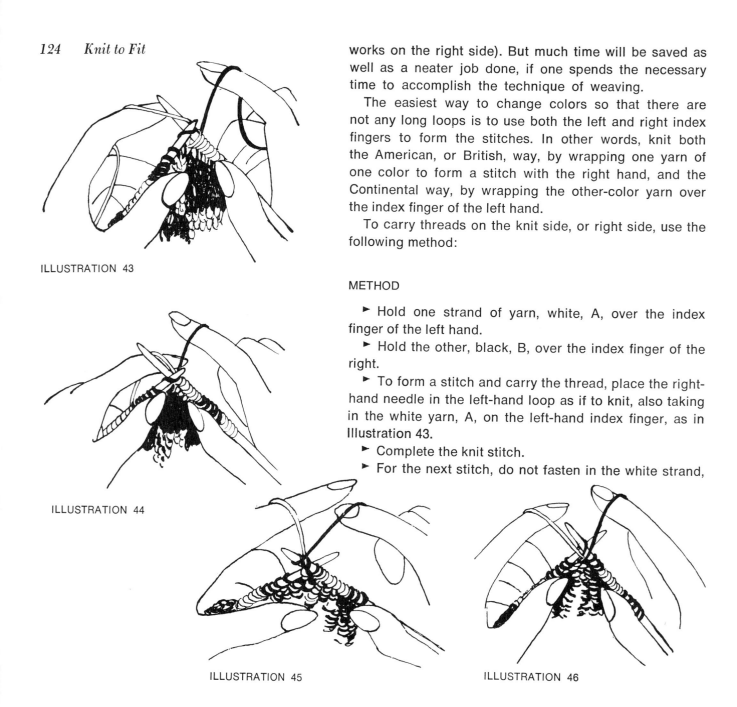

ILLUSTRATION 43

ILLUSTRATION 44

ILLUSTRATION 45

ILLUSTRATION 46

works on the right side). But much time will be saved as well as a neater job done, if one spends the necessary time to accomplish the technique of weaving.

The easiest way to change colors so that there are not any long loops is to use both the left and right index fingers to form the stitches. In other words, knit both the American, or British, way, by wrapping one yarn of one color to form a stitch with the right hand, and the Continental way, by wrapping the other-color yarn over the index finger of the left hand.

To carry threads on the knit side, or right side, use the following method:

METHOD

► Hold one strand of yarn, white, A, over the index finger of the left hand.

► Hold the other, black, B, over the index finger of the right.

► To form a stitch and carry the thread, place the right-hand needle in the left-hand loop as if to knit, also taking in the white yarn, A, on the left-hand index finger, as in Illustration 43.

► Complete the knit stitch.

► For the next stitch, do not fasten in the white strand,

A, but only every 3rd or 4th stitch. There is a tendency to separate the stitches, if done every other stitch. See Illustration 44.

If only two or three stitches are to be made, it is not necessary to catch in the other color. Rather, knit the stitches the Continental way, forming the stitch with the yarn over the left index finger. In knitting many stitches, however, change the black, B, to the left hand, and white, A, to the right.

On the purl side, or wrong side, the principle is the same as the knit stitch, except that you are working on the front side of the work.

METHOD

► Put the needle in as if to purl, catching or fastening in the strand, white, A, on the left-hand index finger. See Illustration 45.

► Complete the purl stitch.

► Do not fasten the thread for the next stitch, but every 3rd or 4th stitch, as for knitting. See Illustration 46.

Work the pattern according to the chart. One square corresponds to a stitch. To know the necessary number of stitches, the number must be divisible by the number for each pattern. See Illustration 47 (twenty-five stitches for one).

To execute Fair Isle or Scandinavian on machine, use the following method: See Illustration 48.

METHOD

1. Place the needles in rest position for color B.
2. Place color-A yarn over all needles, and knit one row.
3. Place all needles in rest position.
4. Return the slide to the beginning of the row.
5. Leave the needles with color-A stitches in rest position.

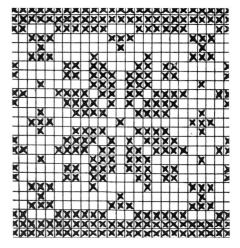

ILLUSTRATION 47

ILLUSTRATION 48

6. Place the needles in previous rest position, in working position.

7. Place color-B yarn over all the needles.

8. Knit one row.

9. Continue the next rows, in the same manner, following the chart for your pattern.

Fancy gold and silver embroidery using sequins, paillettes, bangle beads, and seed pearls are very popular since non-tarnishable metallic threads have been developed. See Illustration 49.

The design is often outlined with one or two strands of metallic thread couched or fastened down with overcast stitches. The centers are sometimes filled with large beads or seed pearls, sequins, or other decorations connected by means of a back stitch and small bead. See Illustration 50.

When rows of sequins or paillettes are desired, buy them in strands and fasten onto the design by means of overcast stitches.

Unattached paillettes may be used by fastening the first by means of a back stitch; then thread the next through the center of the first, etc.

To add sequins to a sweater or hat, use 2 yarns or threads, one finer than the other; thread the thin yarn with the sequins and distribute them at certain desired spaces, when knitting the 2 yarns at the same time. This style allows heavier material to be used for the garment.

21
Accents

ILLUSTRATION 49

ILLUSTRATION 50

TRANSFERRING DESIGNS ON FABRIC

Since knitted material is easily stretched out of shape, either fine canvas or other fine material must be sewn at the back. If needlepoint or cross stitch is used for the decoration, the canvas is attached at the front of the work.

METHOD

1. Mark the position of the design with small pins.
2. Transfer the design with a quick downward press. Be careful of smudging.
3. If making own design, carbon paper may be used in many instances.
4. For fine materials, trace the design on tissue paper, and baste on the right side. Remove the tissue paper after the design has been completed.

There are endless ways of decorating knits—crochet and daisy-knit flowers, appliqués of felt and other material, duplicate stitches, textile painting, and monogramming, to name some of them. See Illustration 51.

If in doubt as to how to apply some of the methods, I suggest you read my *Complete Book of Needlecraft*.

BUTTONS

Crochet

Crochet is worked more easily over wooden forms than over metal, because the work does not slip. Wooden molds may be purchased at notion counters. Remember that the added material adds greatly to the size.

Use a small crochet hook to insure a small stitch, the size depending upon the type of yarn.

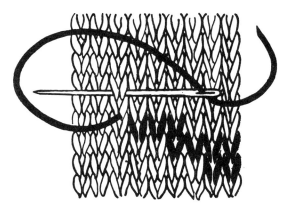

ILLUSTRATION 51

METHOD

1. Chain 4 to 6 stitches and join with a slip-stitch.
2. Single crochet in the ring (about 6 single crochets) until the ring is closed and the work is flat.
3. Mark the beginning of the round, and single crochet twice in each stitch.
4. Continue to increase as many times in each round as single crochet in step 2.
5. When nearing the size of the mold, single crochet one round even. Note that the work must fit very tightly, or it will slip when worn.
6. Place the material over the mold and decrease in each round, the same number of times you increased, more if necessary.
7. To decrease, insert the hook in the chain, draw out the loop (do not finish the stitch); insert the hook in the

next chain, draw out the loop (3 loops on the hook). Thread over and through the 3 loops on the hook.

8. Leave an end to fasten on the garment.

Knitted

Metal molds for knitted material may be obtained at notion departments and many Five-and-Tens.

METHOD

1. Knit a piece of stockinette-stitch material, starting with 4 to 6 stitches, depending upon the weight of the yarn.

2. Increase at the beginning and end of the knit rows until the piece is wide enough.

3. Work 4 to 6 rows even.

4. Decrease just as the increases were done.

5. For completing the button, follow the directions that are given with the molds.

Single crochet over plastic rings

METHOD

1. Single crochet tightly and as closely as possible over the ring.

2. Join.

3. Turn the stitches toward the center and sew together.

4. A bead, shell, or rhinestone may be put in to give added chic.

BELTS

Plastic rings of different sizes may be used instead of buckles for belts. Both are covered with tight, single-

ILLUSTRATION 52

crochet stitches. The belt material should be sewn over grosgrain ribbon to give it strength and a neat edge. If a wide belt is desired, catch a stitch in the center to prevent rolling.

We have diagrammed and charted basic, simple upper garments, with normal shoulders and normal armscyes, with only the fullness added that gives the necessary amount of ease. Now we consider fitted jackets that are large enough to be worn over sweaters, blouses, etc. Take all measurements as explained in Chapter 3, adding the necessary amounts. See Illustration 53.

MEASUREMENTS

Waist

It is advisable not to knit the waist too tightly; therefore, a slight surplus width is necessary. The amount really depends upon individual needs, however. A poor figure should never wear a too tight-fitting garment.

Generally 2 inches for the entire waist is allowed, that is, 1 inch more for the back measurement and 1 inch for the front.

22
Fitted Jackets

Bust

For fitted jackets, no matter what the type of figure, a difference is made between the width of the front and the back.

Use the across-the-back measurement from underarm seam to underarm seam and the front bust measurement from underarm seam to underarm seam, then add 2 inches to the total measurement, that is, 1 inch to the back and 1 inch to the front. More may be added if the figure calls for it. Remember that a large woman with a good figure looks well in fitted clothes; but if too much is added, she appears to be larger.

Armhole or armscye

1 inch is added to the total armscye measurement, as taken in Chapter 3, that is, one-half inch to each one-half armhole measurement.

Underarm to waist

The underarm to waist measurement is one-half inch shorter than the basic sweater measurement; therefore, after measuring from the waist to the armpit, as explained in Chapter 3, 1½ inches are deducted (not 1 inch, as for the sweater).

Shoulder to shoulder

The shoulders for jackets are a little longer, so that an extra garment may be worn underneath.

Allow one-half inch more on each side of the tip of the shoulder, that is, 1 inch more than the measurement that was taken from the tip to the tip.

Sleeve underarm length

The sleeve underarm length is one-half inch shorter because of the larger armscye; therefore, 1½ inches are deducted from the wrist to the armpit measurement (not 1 inch as in the case of sweaters).

Length of jacket

This depends entirely upon the figure, as did the length of the cardigan.

The following chart gives an example of changes:

SWEATER	JACKET
Waist—26 inches	26 inches + 2 is 28 inches
Across the back—18 inches	18 inches + 1 is 19 inches
Front bust—19 inches	19 inches + 1 is 20 inches
Underarm to waist—8 inches	8 inches − ½ inch is 7½ inches
Shoulder to shoulder— 14½ inches	14½ inches + 1 inch is 15½ inches
Sleeve underarm length— 18 inches	18 inches − ½ inch is 17½ inches
Wrist—6 inches	6 inches
Upper arm—11 inches	11 inches
Armscye—18 inches	18 inches + 1 inch is 19 inches

▶ PROJECT ◀

▶ *With a woman's measurements, as in Chapter 6, the across the back underarm—17½ inches—and the front bust measurement—18½ inches—state the difference in measurements between a jacket and a basic sweater.*

▶ *Check answers on page 232.*

DARTS

Darts, whether used in sewing or knitting, are to add or take out width, so that the garment may curve where

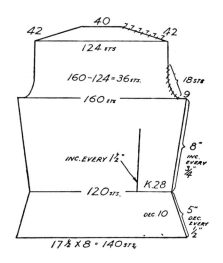

DIAGRAM 59

necessary. The aim of a well-fitting garment is to give the appearance of being molded to the figure.

It is indeed possible to make darts when knitting. The surplus width is taken out by decreasing, and extra width is added by increasing at the correct places.

Vertical waist darts

Vertical darts are knitted at right angles to the waist and hip lines and give form to the garments. They should be knitted on a line with the shoulder blades at the back and with the bust in front. The height and depth of the dart varies with the individual.

In a fitted jacket, if all the stitches were decreased or increased at the sides, points would be formed at the underarm seams, and blocking would not alter the effect.

Shoulder darts

The purpose of the shoulder dart is to eliminate some of the surplus width that was necessary for the curve of the bust. In inexpensive clothes, a larger amount is taken out at the armhole; but this gives a very poor fit.

The shoulder dart is generally placed in the center of the shoulder and tapers gradually toward the fullest point of the bust. In a fitted jacket, where the shoulder measurement is 1 inch longer, the extra stitches are not used for the back of the neck.

MEASUREMENTS

Half the waist—15 inches
The back underarm measurement—20 inches
The front bust measurement—22 inches
Underarm to waist—8 inches
Hips (5 inches down)—35 inches

Stitch gauge—8 stitches to the inch

EXAMPLE

For the back:

► Bottom to waist, see Diagram 59.
► Half the waist is 15 inches times 8 stitches to the inch = 120 stitches.
► The across the back measurement is 20 inches times 8 stitches to the inch = 160 stitches.
► The difference between 160 stitches and 120 stitches is 40 stitches to increase from the waist to the underarm.
► Divide by 4, which is 10 stitches to increase at each side and 10 stitches to add at 2 vertical waist darts.
► Increase 10 stitches in each dart, 2 stitches at a time, every 1½ inches and 10 stitches at each side, every three-quarters inch.
► Follow the diagram. No shoulder dart is necessary. The vertical dart is placed about one-quarter of the distance of the waist measurement. Place a marker at this point; then the dart is made by increasing in a stitch, K. 1, before the marker, then K. 1 and increasing a stitch after the marker, i.e., knit 28 stitches, increase in a stitch, K. 1 marker, K. 1 increase in a stitch.

EXAMPLE

For the front:

► Across the front bust—22 inches. Half is 11 inches, times 8 stitches to the inch = 88 stitches. So both the front and back side shaping are the same. Increase 10 stitches at the side, allowing 18 stitches to be increased in a dart.

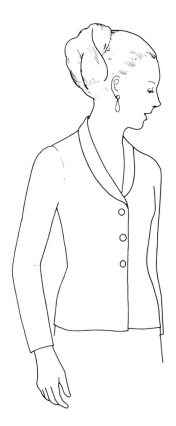

ILLUSTRATION 53

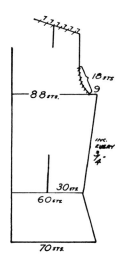

DIAGRAM 60

▶ Place the marker at half the waist measurement, 30 stitches, then increase before and after the marker 9 times, every three-quarters inch, at the same time increasing at the side, 10 times.

▶ Shoulder dart: Because there are 8 extra stitches at the front, these 8 stitches must be decreased in a dart toward the center of the shoulder. Place a marker after the 25th stitch and decrease instead of increasing every inch, 4 times. Note that 21 stitches is the center of the shoulder, but 4 stitches have to be added to allow for decreasing at one side of the dart, making 25 stitches. See Diagram 60. If a line were drawn, the vertical dart would meet the shoulder dart.

▶ **PROJECT** ◀

▶ *Diagram and chart the back and front of a fitted jacket using the same measurements as the example, but with 7 stitches to the inch.*

▶ *Check answers on pages 232 and 233.*

Every vacation wardrobe requires a shortie coat. As figure, taste, and purse vary, so does the type of coat that one conjures up in one's mind. All, however, must have the important qualities of design and good workmanship.

As shortie coats are very often carried, they must not be heavy or cumbersome. They must be fashioned so that they are appropriate from early morning until the wee hours of the night. Such a coat is indeed possible, especially if it is hand knitted. A knitted coat involves no fuss or muss, and it is ready at any hour of the day—whether it has reclined on a luggage rack, in a drawer, or been slung over one's arm. See Illustration 54.

There are many types of shortie coats.

▶ Squared box-jacket, cropped short just below the waist. (No protruding behind for this length: make the coat longer if the figure is not too good.)

▶ Hip-length coats with three-quarter wide sleeves.

▶ Short coats with a gentle flare, or, wider ones if desired.

▶ Raglan sleeved coats, hip-length or longer to suit individual needs.

23
Shortie Coats

ILLUSTRATION 54

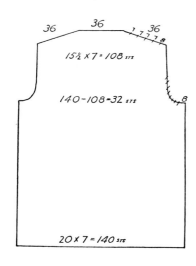

DIAGRAM 61

I want to emphasize one thing particularly. No wide short coat should ever be worn with a very full skirt, no matter what type of figure. It takes away from the slimness of a pretty silhouette and adds considerable weight to the large person. Too-wide shoulders are not good either. For all purposes, the extra inch for shoulders as for jackets is all that is needed.

The same applies to capes; however, in a short cape, there is a break in the silhouette, where a slim waist breaks the lines.

SQUARED BOX-JACKET

Without any added instructions, you should almost be able to diagram this type.

METHOD

► A box coat generally has straight lines, so the width at the bottom is the same as the across-the-back-underarm measurement.

► 2 inches is generally sufficient to add to the across-the-back-underarm measurement that was taken in Chapter 6 for sweaters. More may be added for a roomier coat.

► Test the width at the bottom.

► In the front, the coat has a high, round neckline, so 6 extra stitches are added to each front for an overlap of 12 stitches for buttons and buttonholes.

► The extra 8 stitches for each front are reduced by a shoulder dart as in Chapter 22. Follow Diagrams 61 and 62.

MEASUREMENTS

Across-the-back-underarm—18 inches plus 2 inches = 20 inches.

Front bust—20 inches plus 2 inches = 22 inches.

Armscye—18 inches plus 2 inches = 20 inches, more if desired.

Shoulder-to-shoulder—14½ inches plus 1 inch = 15½ inches.

Length of coat from the underarm—10 to 14 inches.

Stitch Gauge—7 stitches to the inch.

Sleeve

Width at the bottom—12 inches.

Width at the upper arm—16 inches.

Length—17 inches.

Cap—6½ inches deep or more.

Diagram 63 is self-explanatory.

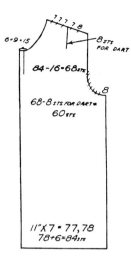

DIAGRAM 62

▶ *PROJECT* ◀

▶ *Diagram and chart a box coat using the following measurements:*

Across-the-back underarm—22 inches.
6 stitches allowed for the overlap in front.
The front bust measurement—24 inches.
Sleeve—three-quarter sleeve, 14 inches long, 13 inches at the bottom, widening to 15 inches.
The other measurements the same as the example.

Stitch gauge—7 stitches to the inch.

▶ *Check answers on pages 234 and 235.*

HIP-LENGTH COAT

This coat has wide, three-quarter sleeves, with slight fullness at the back, and is fitted from the underarm. It

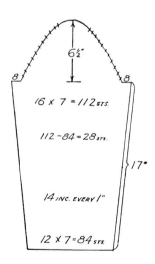

DIAGRAM 63

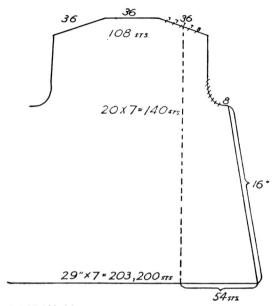

36   36   36
108 sts.
20 x 7 = 140 sts
8
16"
29" x 7 = 203,200 sts
54 sts

DIAGRAM 64

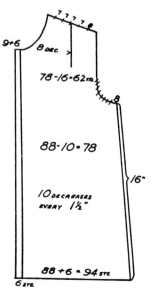

9+6   8 dec.
7 7 7 8
78-16-62 m.
8
88-10-78
16"
10 decreases every 1½"
88+6 = 94 sts.
6 sts.

DIAGRAM 65

is always better to chart the back first, because the sides of the back and front must be shaped the same. Also the shoulders must fit, making darts at the front shoulders necessary. Follow Diagrams 64 and 65.

MEASUREMENTS

Width at the bottom—back—29 inches.
Width at the bottom—front—25 inches.
Length from the underarm—16 inches.
Armhole—21 inches.
Sleeve—14 inches long, shaped from 13 inches to 16 inches.

EXAMPLE

▶ Width at the bottom—29 inches times 7 stitches to the inch = 203 stitches, 200 stitches for even 10's.

▶ Across-the-back-underarm—20 inches times 7 stitches to the inch = 140 stitches.

▶ 200 stitches minus 140 stitches leaves 60 stitches to decrease to the armscye.

▶ The length of the coat to the underarm seam is 16 inches. Allowing for 2 flares as well as decreasing at the sides, 6 into 60 makes 10 decreases, every 1½ inches at the sides, and 20 stitches to decrease in each flare, making 40 stitches—60 stitches altogether.

▶ To locate the position of the flares, work as follows:

The center of the shoulder is 18 stitches.
Plus 16 stitches to take off for the armhole.
Plus 10 stitches to decrease at the underarm seam.
Plus 10 stitches to decrease for half a flare, makes a total of 54 stitches.

Therefore, place 2 markers, marking the position of the 2 flares, which are 54 stitches from each end.

This is the nearest position of the flares; more stitches may be added if the fullness is desired toward the back.

► For darts, only 1 stitch was allotted before and after the marker. Here, it is better to leave 6 stitches, so that the flare will have a better shape. The first decrease at 1½ inches will be:

Knit to within 8 stitches of the marker.
Knit 2 together. Knit 6 stitches.
Move the marker. Knit 6 stitches. Knit 2 together.
Work in the same way for the other flare, decreasing 2 stitches each time, every 1½ inches, as on the sides.

► For a very wide back, decreases could be made in the same way as for a full skirt, decreasing 10 or 20 stitches at a time.
► The front is diagrammed in the same way as the box coat, except that the side seams are decreased as on the back.
► The sleeve is self-explanatory. (See Diagram 66.)

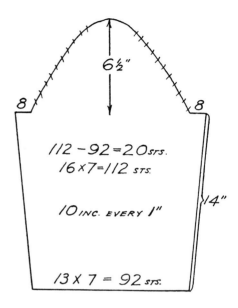

DIAGRAM 66

SHORT COAT WITH WIDER BACK

The back has three flares. On this type of coat, the flares do not stop at the underarm, but continue to about 5 inches below the tip of the shoulder. (If they continued all the way, the shoulders would droop.)

MEASUREMENTS

    Width at the bottom—37 inches
    Underarm seam—18 inches
    Armscye—22 inches
    Remainder—the same measurements as the hip-
        length coat.

        Stitch gauge—7 sts. to the inch

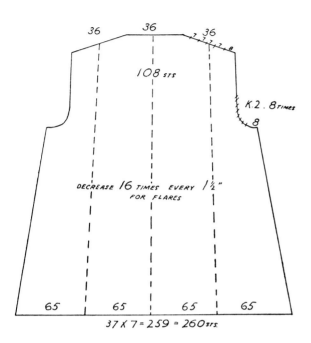

DIAGRAM 67

EXAMPLE

► The front is the same as Diagram 64, so the decreasing at the side seams is 12 decreases every 1½ inches.

► The center of the shoulder is 18 stitches, plus 16 stitches to take off for the armscye, plus 16 stitches to decrease for one half flare, plus 12 stitches to decrease at the side seam, making a total of 62 stitches.

► There are 3 flares (see Diagram 67) and 4 spaces; 4 into 260 stitches goes 65 times, approximately 62 stitches; therefore, place the markers at every 65th stitch, and decrease every 1½ inches, as for previous coat.

RAGLANS

Consider the top of a raglan-sleeved short coat in the same light as a raglan sweater with set-in sleeves, knitting the back first, then the fronts, and finally the sleeves, as in the directions for the previous shortie coat. Complete the raglans as for raglans with set-in sleeves, Chapter 12.

► PROJECT ◄

► *Spend considerable time absorbing the mathematics used in shortie coats.*

RIBBON

Block each piece made of ribbon separately, according to the measurements, before sewing them together, then flatten the seams. Be very careful not to stretch the armscye, neckline, etc. Turn to Chapters 5 and 30 to refresh your memory.

Steaming or blocking is easier when garments are made of other materials, such as yarn, cotton, wool-yarn-and-cotton, linen yarns, and metallics, when they are crocheted together.

JACKETS

Turn to Chapter 13. The same principles apply to blocking jackets as to blocking sweaters, with the exception of the side seams and the two fronts. So follow the same directions up to step 9, adding at step 5 the waist-to-bottom-of-the-jacket measurement, and the across-the-hip measurement (of the jacket). Do not forget to use the

24
Blocking Jackets and Shortie Coats

measurements for the jacket, which differ from the sweater measurements.

METHOD

10. Pin down one center front, allowing for extra width and overlap.
11. Adjust half the neckline and pin in position.
12. Pin down the other center front, allowing for extra width and overlap.
13. Adjust the other half neckline.

Continue with steps 12 through 17.

SHORTIE COATS

We have knitted to the measurement of the finished garment; so the blocking is easy, and there is absolutely no guesswork as there is when following measurements of so-called sizes 32, 34, etc.

The garments have the shape and correct size desired, and there is no possibility of having to overstretch for fit. Now you realize why the stitch gauge and measurements are very important.

Shortie coats are blocked in the same manner as jackets; but it is possible that blocking—in the sense of pinning to the board—is not necessary. Just steam flat with a steam iron.

Lining

It may be that one would like a lined jacket. Of course, we have no actual paper pattern. We do have our measurements; but for the layman I would suggest basting the coat with fairly close basting stitches, then steaming or blocking it. Pull out the basting threads and use the pieces for a paper pattern, allowing ⅜-inch seams. In this way the fit of the lining is assured.

Cuffs

If one would like cuffs on the bottom of the sleeves, one-half inch more stitches should be allowed at the beginning (make separately). Then increase at both sides, every other row, or every 4th row, according to desired increase. Make the cuffs as wide as desired, 3, 4, or 5 inches.

The joining of the cuff is not sewn to the center of the wrist, but a little more toward the back, on a line with the elbow—actually one-third of the remaining one-half.

Collar

The same applies to a large stand-up collar; but this time, pick up the stitches instead of sewing on afterwards, as in the case of the cuffs.

▶ PROJECT ◀

► *Now you are ready to block anything. Test your ability.*

Facings

I have found that knitted facings are often too bulky. For all general purposes, I suggest grosgrain ribbon, which has a picot edge, and makes handling easier. The ribbon should be shrunk before using, either with a damp cloth and warm iron, or a steam iron.

As I suggested for sweaters, the garment should be first steamed to flatten the material, then the measurement taken for the facing either on the person or a dress-form, allowing 1 inch extra for turn-ins.

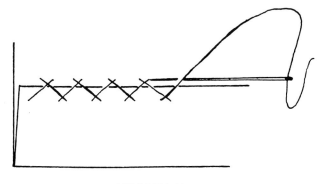

DIAGRAM 68

For jackets and coats where wide facings are necessary for the collar, lapels, and down the fronts, any lining material that a dressmaker usually uses is all right. The pieces for the collar and the lapels should be slightly smaller to allow for the turn-down or roll, and all pieces should be cut straight on the grain of the material.

Before cutting the material smaller, test around the hand for the desired roll.

Catch-stitch in a zig-zag manner on both the lining for the collar and the lapels. See Diagram 68.

To strengthen the shoulder line, seam binding may be sewn to the shoulder seams and across the back of the neck to prevent sagging.

Now we have arrived at one of the big reasons why women with figures that do not fall into an exact pattern size consider hand-knits absolutely "out" for them: There have been too many protruding behinds and figure problems stressed. The real fault rests with the instructor or designer; for, with a well-fitting foundation and a correctly styled garment, any woman can look well in a hand-knit.

There are far too many people instructing in hand-knitting who do not know the first thing about dress design: how to take measurements for knits, diagramming and charting, or correct styling to meet individual needs. Practically all their instructions are guesswork, through the use of only a knitting manual, in which individual needs cannot be taken into consideration. I feel it is appalling the way some "knit shops" cut and hack hand-knits, especially ribbons. Indeed, in some instances, an exorbitant price is charged for such so-called altering and finishing.

25
Skirts

SKIRT STYLING

There are 5 factors to be considered in a well-fitting skirt.

► The skirt should be wide enough at the hips to allow for comfortable sitting.

► Every skirt should have extra width at the hip line no matter what the style or for what type of figure it is made. The width varies with the style, but a general rule is: the slimmer the lines, the greater the amount to be added. The reason for slim skirts "reaching up" when one is sitting is that sufficient room is not allowed for so-called "spreading." The *width*, not the *length*, is at fault—and no amount of length that is added will change the fact.

► A skirt should allow for freedom of movement. Any garment should be considered in the light of sitting, standing, and walking.

► The style should be suited to the purpose: day, afternoon, evening, etc.

► The grain—that is, the rows of knitting—should run horizontally around the figure and should be straight up and down.

Length of skirt

As is clear today in the constantly changing world of fashion, hemlines may extend to all lengths.

Mini.   May be anywhere from 6 to 10 inches above the knee.

Kneecapper.   To the knee, bent, or a little lower.

Midi-length.   Halfway down the calf.

Maxi.   To the floor, center of front foot, or two inches above the floor.

SHIFTS

Shifts, of course, are simply a combination of a skirt and upper garment. Actually, the original word was "chemise," which was an undergarment or lingerie in the British Isles in the nineties. Only the lowly called them "shifts" at that time.

Naturally there are some that fit and some that hang loosely. The fit depends greatly upon the figure. For the slender figure, the loose-fitting shifts are fine, using the bust measurement for width. As for sweaters, etc., 4 inches should be added to the actual bust measurement; and the armhole, shoulders, and neckline should be figured using the same method as that for a sleeveless sweater. If caps or sleeves are desired, consider the same method as that for sweaters with caps or sleeves.

Be careful the underarm-to-waist measurement is not too long. If no opening is allowed in front, a long zipper is necessary at the center back; and a side, long zipper is essential for a fitted garment.

If a fitted shift is desired, use instructions for the appropriate type of skirt and continue for the fitted top.

26
Straight Skirts

For straight skirts, the following measurements are necessary.

Waist. The waist is taken with 2 fingers eased between the tape and the body. This is one measurement that fits. See Chapter 3.

Hips. This is not the actual hip measurement, but around the fullest part, 7 to 9 inches down, the same distance from the waist all the way around. Do not pull the tape tightly, but eased, as when measuring for a pattern. Be particularly careful, especially for a larger person with a "tummy." The skirt must not draw in front.

Width at the bottom. This varies. The necessary hip measurement may be used, in which case a slit or pleat is necessary. A wider bottom is still considered a straight skirt, but no slit is required.

METHOD

1. Deduct 1 inch from the length for the crocheting at the top and bottom.

2. Multiply the waist, the necessary hip measurement, and the width at the bottom by the stitch gauge.

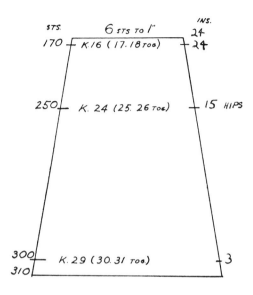

6 sts to the inch

Sts		Ins	
170		24	
170	K.16 (17.18 tog.)	24	last inch even
180	K.17 (18.19 tog.)	23	
190	K.18 (19.20 tog.)	22	
200	K.19 (20.21 tog.)	21	
210	K.20 (21.22 tog.)	20	
220	K.21 (22.23 tog.)	19	
230	K.22 (23.24 tog.)	18	
240	K.23 (24.25 tog.)	17	
250	K.24 (25.26 tog.)	15	Hips
260	K.25 (26.27 tog.)	13	
270	K.26 (27.28 tog.)	11	
280	K.27 (28.29 tog.)	9	
290	K.28 (29.30 tog.)	6	
300	K.29 (30.31 tog.)	3	
310			

DIAGRAM 69

3. Use the nearest numbers, divisible by 10, to simplify the charting.

4. Subtract the necessary stitches at the hip from the stitches at the bottom, then from the hip to the waist.

5. Divide by 10 to learn how many decreases are to be made.

6. Divide the number of decreases into the number of inches from the bottom to the hip and from the hip to the waist to know where to decrease. Any extra inches are to be added, 1 inch at a time, to the decreases nearest the bottom and then the hips.

No matter what amount of stretch has been allowed for certain materials, the garment must be charted correctly. When measuring, allow for the stretch.

MEASUREMENTS

Waist—28 inches.
Hip—38 inches, 9 inches below the waist.
Length—25 inches, 1 inch allowed for crocheting, so 24 inches is the knitted length.
Width at the bottom—52 inches.

Stitch Gauge—6 stitches to the inch.

Note that 4 inches are added to the hip measurement to allow for "spread."

EXAMPLE

▶ Waist—28 inches times 6 stitches to the inch = 168 stitches; the nearest number divisible by 10 is 170 stitches.

▶ Hips—38 inches plus 4 inches = 42 inches, times 6 is 252 stitches; the nearest 10 is 250 stitches.

▶ Width at the bottom—52 inches times 6 = 312 stitches; the nearest 10 is 310 stitches.

To decrease from the bottom to the hip, follow the example on page 155.

EXAMPLE

➤ 310 stitches minus 250 stitches leaves 60 stitches to be reduced evenly to the hips.

➤ Decreasing 10 stitches at a time, there are 6 decreases.

➤ 25 inches is the finished length, but 24 inches the knitted length; therefore, the hip, 9 inches down, is 15 inches.

➤ 15 inches to make 6 decreases of 10 stitches.

➤ 6 into 21 goes 3 times and 3 inches over.

➤ Therefore, the first 3 decreases are at every 3 inches and the next 3 are 2 inches apart. Follow diagram.

In 310 stitches there are 31 tens to be reduced to 30 tens. This is done by knitting 29 stitches and the 30th and 31st stitches together all the way around.

The next number is automatically reduced 1 stitch, so the next decrease is knit 28 stitches and the 29th and 30th together, and so on for the remainder of the decreasing.

250 stitches at the hips minus 170 stitches at the waist = 80 stitches or 8 decreases of 10.

The last decrease is never at the waistline. Allow one-half inch or 1 inch even.

▶ *PROJECT* ◀

➤ *Diagram and chart a straight skirt with the following measurements:*

Waist—28 inches.
Hip—38 inches, 9 inches down.
Length of skirt—25 inches, allow 1 inch for crocheting.
Width at the bottom—10 inches more than the hip measurement—52 inches.

▶ *Check answers on pages 235 and 236.*

STRAIGHT TWO-PIECE SKIRT ON MACHINE

The same measurements are used as in Diagram 69. For a well-fitting, 2-piece skirt, the decreases must be made across a row.

Follow the diagrams.

MEASUREMENTS

Bottom—½ of 310 stitches = 155 stitches
Hips   —½ of 250 stitches = 125 stitches
Waist   —½ of 170 stitches = 85 stitches

The decreases are exactly the same as those for working on a circular needle, except that half the stitches will be taken off each time, which means that not 10 but 5 stitches are decreased at a time, allowing, of course, rows for inches.

Remember that extra stitches should be allowed for seam allowances. I suggest 2 or 3 at each side.

The first decrease is K. 29, then 30 and 31 together, and so on. However, for a better fit, the first 29 stitches may be split and have K. 15, then 16 and 17 together. At the end, there will be K. 14, and so on up the skirt, allowing one fewer stitch between every decrease.

To decrease across a row, use the following method:

METHOD

1. Work an extra row using a contrasting color where decreases must be made.

2. Drop the work from the machine.

3. Fold so that the main-color stitches stand out.

4. Replace on the machine, putting 2 stitches on one needle where decreases are required, being sure all latches are open.

5. Pull out contrasting color.

To increase across a row, increase in the same way but leave a space open for extra stitch.

See answers on pages 235 and 236.

DIFFERENT STITCH GAUGES AND LENGTHS

Longer length

MEASUREMENTS

The same as for previous straight skirt.

> Length of Skirt—28 inches.
> Knitted Length—27 inches.
>
> Stitch Gauge—7 stitches to the inch.

EXAMPLE

▶ Waist—28 inches times 7 stitches to the inch = 196 stitches, nearest 10, 200 stitches.

▶ Hip—38 inches plus 4 inches =· 42 inches, times 7 stitches to the inch is 294 stitches, nearest 10, 290 stitches for the hip (8 inches down).

▶ Width at the bottom—52 inches times 7 stitches to the inch = 364 stitches, nearest 10, 360 stitches.

▶ Diagram 70 is self-explanatory. Follow closely.

Shorter length

MEASUREMENTS

The measurements are the same as for the previous example.

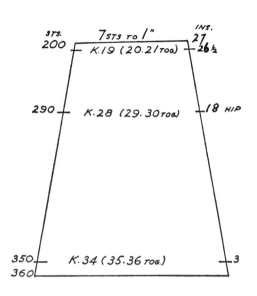

7 sts to the inch

Sts		Ins	
200		27	last 1/2 inch even
200	K.19 (20.21 tog.)	26 1/2	
210	K.20 (21.22 tog.)	26	
220	K.21 (22.23 tog.)	25	
230	K.22 (23.24 tog.)	24	
240	K.23 (24.25 tog.)	23	
250	K.24 (25.26 tog.)	22	
260	K.25 (26.27 tog.)	21	
270	K.26 (27.28 tog.)	20	
280	K.27 (28.29 tog.)	19	
290	K.28 (29.30 tog.)	18	Hip
300	K.29 (30.31 tog.)	16	
310	K.30 (31.32 tog.)	14	
320	K.31 (32.33 tog.)	12	
330	K.32 (33.34 tog.)	9	
340	K.33 (34.35 tog.)	6	
350	K.34 (35.36 tog.)	3	
360			

DIAGRAM 70

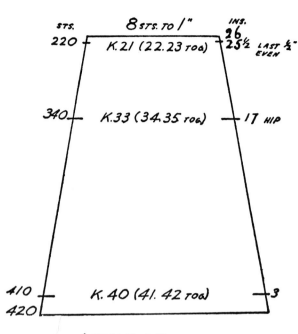

8 sts to the inch

Sts		Ins	
220		26	last 1/2 inch even
220	K.21 (22.23 tog.)	25 1/2	
230	K.22 (23.24 tog.)	25	
240	K.23 (24.25 tog.)	24 1/2	
250	K.24 (25.26 tog.)	24	
260	K.25 (26.27 tog.)	23 1/2	
270	K.26 (27.28 tog.)	23	
280	K.27 (28.29 tog.)	22 1/2	
290	K.28 (29.30 tog.)	22	
300	K.29 (30.31 tog.)	21	
310	K.30 (31.32 tog.)	20	
320	K.31 (32.33 tog.)	19	
330	K.32 (33.34 tog.)	18	
340	K.33 (34.35 tog.)	17	Hip
350	K.34 (35.36 tog.)	15	
360	K.35 (36.37 tog.)	13	
370	K.36 (37.38 tog.)	11	
380	K.37 (38.39 tog.)	9	
390	K.38 (39.40 tog.)	7	
400	K.39 (40.41 tog.)	5	
410	K.40 (41.42 tog.)	3	
420			

DIAGRAM 71

Length of Skirt—27 inches.
Knitted Length—26 inches.

Stitch Gauge—8 stitches to the inch.

EXAMPLE

► Waist—28 inches times 8 stitches to the inch = 224 stitches, nearest 10, 220 stitches.

► Hip—38 inches plus 4 inches = 42 inches times 8 stitches to the inch is 336 stitches, 340 stitches for the hip (9 inches down).

► Width at the bottom—52 inches times 8 stitches to the inch is 416 stitches, nearest 10, 420 stitches. Follow Diagram 71.

► PROJECT ◄

► *Diagram and chart 2 straight skirts, using the same measurements as those used above.*

Waist—28 inches.
Hip—38 inches at the fullest part (9 inches below the waist).
Length of skirt—30 inches.

Stitch Gauge—7 and 8 stitches to the inch.

MACHINE-KNIT SKIRT IN TWO PIECES

This method has six edges for increasing, with open darts starting at the top. You will note that when sewing, darts are made where necessary, but generally over one-third is allowed at the center for knitting. There are no seam allowances at the sides.

METHOD

Three balls are necessary for this procedure.

Starting from left to right, cast on 24 sts.; leave 14 sts. at rest; cast on 36 sts. for the center; 14 sts. at rest; cast on 24 sts. 126 sts., from side to side, are in operation.

Work 1 inch even, then increase on all 6 sides, every inch, until all the spaces are filled and there are 126 sts.

Knit evenly for the desired length.

Knit 2 similar pieces.

See answers on page 236.

MEASUREMENTS

Waist—28 inches
Hip—38 inches
Length—30 inches

Stitch Gauge—6 stitches to the inch

EXAMPLE

► Half of Waist, 28 inches, is 14 inches.

► Half of necessary hip, 42 inches, is 21 inches.

► 14 inches × by 6 stitches to the inch = 84 stitches (waist).

► 21 inches × by 6 stitches to the inch = 126 stitches. (hip).

► The difference—126 stitches minus 84 means 42 stitches to be added—2 stitches at each dart and 1 stitch at each side, making 6 increases.

► 6 into 42 stitches goes 7 times; therefore, 7 increases altogether.

► Increase both in darts and sides, every inch, 7 times; then work straight for the desired length on the 126 stitches. See Diagram 72.

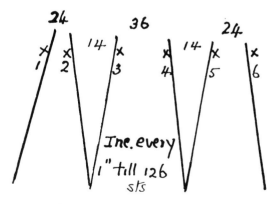

DIAGRAM 72

Actually the darts should not be quite so long or curve as much as the side shaping, although the above directions will suffice. The following is a second way for making darts.

EXAMPLE

► Allow about 5 inches for each dart. So, increasing for darts, every inch for 5 inches, requires 5 × 4, which = 20 stitches.

► 42 stitches minus 20 stitches leaves 22 stitches for both sides, or 11 for each side.

► The hip is 9 inches down from the waist; so increase every three-quarter inch, 11 times at the sides, until you have 126 stitches.

The fullness that is added at the hips of a flared skirt depends upon the amount of flare from the bottom to the hips. Some flared skirts may appear to fit around the hips; but, even then, there must be at least 2 inches more allowed for the actual hip measurement. Generally speaking, the smaller the flare, the greater the amount added at the hips. If the width at the bottom, for example, is only 15 inches more than the actual hip measurement, this is a semi-straight skirt; and 4 inches more than the hip measurement should be added. For small figures, a loose-fitting skirt from the bottom to the waist may be more desirable, with the decreasing figured accordingly—even all the way from the bottom to the waist.

27
Flared Skirts

SKIRT WITH EVEN FLARE TO THE HIPS

We shall again use the measurements that were used for the straight skirt.

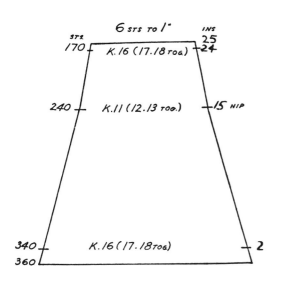

6 sts to the inch

Sts		Ins	
170		25	
170	K.16 (17.18 tog.)	24	last inch even
180	K.17 (18.19 tog.)	23	
190	K.18 (19.20 tog.)	22	
200	K.19 (20.21 tog.)	20	
210	K.20 (21.22 tog.)	19	
220	K.21 (22.23 tog.)	18	
230	K.22 (23.24 tog.)	17	
240	K.11 (12.13 tog.)	15	Hip
260	K.12 (13.14 tog.)	12	
280	K.13 (14.15 tog.)	9	
300	K.14 (15.16 tog.)	6	
320	K.15 (16.17 tog.)	4	
340	K.16 (17.18 tog.)	2	
360			

DIAGRAM 73

MEASUREMENTS

Waist—28 inches.
Hips—38 inches.
Length—31 inches.
Width at the Bottom—60 inches.

Stitch Gauge—6 stitches to the inch.

In our example, 20 inches were added to the width at the bottom, so only 2 inches more than the actual hip measurement are necessary, as there is sufficient width below the hips.

EXAMPLE

► Waist—28 inches times 6 stitches to the inch = 168 stitches, even 10 is 170 stitches.

► Hips—38 inches plus 2 inches = 40 inches times 6 is 240 stitches.

► Width at the bottom—40 inches plus 20 inches = 60 inches times 6 = 360 stitches. Follow Diagram 73.

► If many stitches are to be decreased, it is better to decrease 20 stitches in one round rather than 10 stitches. To take off 20 stitches, the number must be divisible by 20; if not, reduce 10 stitches first.

► In 360, there are 18 twenties. For 340, we require 17 twenties; therefore, every 18 stitches have to be decreased 1 stitch. That is, knit 16 stitches, then knit the 17th and 18th together.

► As in the straight skirt, the number of stitches between each decrease automatically decreases 1 stitch at a time. See the straight skirt for the method of ascertaining the position of decreases.

► The difference in the number of stitches from the bottom to the hips is 120 stitches or 6 decreases of 20 stitches. 6 into 21 goes 3 inches with 3 inches over;

therefore, the first 3 decreases are at every 2 inches and the remainder at 3 inches to the hips.

From the hips to the waist, decrease so that 240 minus 170 stitches leaves 70; therefore, there are 7 decreases of 10 stitches. So decrease every inch, 7 times, with the last inch even.

▶ PROJECT ◀

▶ *Diagram and chart a flared skirt using measurements as for Chapter 26, allowing 1 inch for crocheting. The width at the bottom is 61 inches, which is 20 inches more than the necessary hip measurement of 39 inches plus 2. The stitch gauge is 6 stitches to the inch.*
▶ *Check the answer on pages 238 through 241.*

DIFFERENT STITCH GAUGES AND LENGTHS

As flared skirts should never be knitted of heavy material, we shall not consider 5 stitches to the inch.

Longer version

Use the example above, allowing a 15-inch flare.

MEASUREMENTS

Length of Skirt—28 inches.
Knitted Length—27 inches.

Stitch Gauge—7 stitches to the inch.

EXAMPLE

▶ Follow Diagram 74.

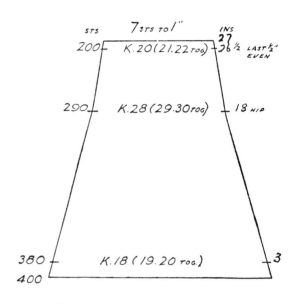

7 sts to the inch

Sts		Ins
200		27
200	K.19 (20.21 tog.)	26 1/2-last 1/2 inch even
210	K.20 (21.22 tog.)	26
220	K.21 (22.23 tog.)	25
230	K.22 (23.24 tog.)	24
240	K.23 (24.25 tog.)	23
250	K.24 (25.26 tog.)	22
260	K.25 (26.27 tog.)	21
270	K.26 (27.28 tog.)	20
280	K.27 (28.29 tog.)	19
290	K.28 (29.30 tog.)	18 Hip
300	K.14 (15.16 tog.)	15
320	K.15 (16.17 tog.)	12
340	K.16 (17.18 tog.)	9
360	K.17 (18.19 tog.)	6
380	K.18 (19.20 tog.)	3
400		

DIAGRAM 74

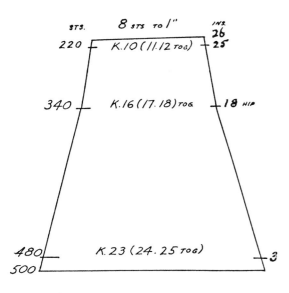

8 sts to the inch

Sts		Ins	
220		26	
220	K.10 (11.12 tog.)	25	Last inch even
240	K.11 (12.13 tog.)	24	
260	K.12 (13.14 tog.)	23	
280	K.13 (14.15 tog.)	22	
300	K.14 (15.16 tog.)	21	
320	K.15 (16.17 tog.)	20	
340	K.16 (17.18 tog.)	18	Hip
360	K.17 (18.19 tog.)	16	
380	K.18 (19.20 tog.)	14	
400	K.19 (20.21 tog.)	12	
420	K.20 (21.22 tog.)	10	
440	K.21 (22.23 tog.)	8	
460	K.22 (23.24 tog.)	6	
480	K.23 (24.25 tog.)	3	
500			

DIAGRAM 75

▶ Waist—28 inches times 7 stitches to the inch = 196 stitches, 200 stitches nearest 10.

▶ Hip—38 inches plus 4 inches = 42 inches times 7 stitches to the inch, or 294 stitches, nearest 10, 290 stitches (9 inches down).

▶ Width at the bottom—42 inches plus 15 inches = 57 inches times 7 stitches to the inch or 399 stitches, nearest 10, 400 stitches.

▶ 400 stitches at the bottom, minus 290 stitches at the hips leaves 110 stitches; therefore, there are 5 decreases of 20 stitches and one decrease of 10 stitches to the hips. (Always check the stitch gauge at the hips.)

▶ 6 times to decrease into 18 inches goes 3; therefore, there are 3 inches between each decrease to the hips.

▶ The stitches from the hips to the waist are taken off in 10's, 9 decreases altogether.

Second version

The flare is released toward the bottom, so that 4 inches is added to the hip measurement.

Use the same measurements as previously.

MEASUREMENTS

Length of Skirt—27 inches.

Knitted Length—26 inches.

Stitch Gauge—8 stitches to the inch.

EXAMPLE

▶ Waist—28 inches times 8 stitches to the inch = 224 stitches, 220 stitches is the nearest 10.

▶ Hips—38 inches plus 4 inches = 42 inches, times 8 stitches to the inch or 336 stitches, 340 stitches is the nearest 10 (8 inches down).

► Bottom of the skirt—42 inches plus 20 inches = 62 inches, times 8 stitches to the inch or 496 stitches, 500 stitches is the nearest 10.

► Study Diagram 75.

▶ *PROJECTS* ◀

► *Using previous measurements and 7 and 8 stitches to the inch gauges, adding 15 inches for 7 stitches to the inch and 20 inches for 8 stitches to the inch, chart the two flared skirts.*

► *Check the answers on pages 238 to 241.*

A gored skirt in hand-knitting is not worked in separate pieces, except for ribbon knits. The effect of gores is achieved by means of purl stitches, 1 or 2, as desired, between each gore.

Gored skirts may have many numbers of gores, 4, 6, 8, 10, and more, depending upon the effect desired, the width at the bottom and individual needs. Again it must be remembered that the figure is very important. A tall, thin person certainly should not have many narrow gores, or, on the other hand, a large person should not have wide gores, especially around the body—this emphasizes width.

A gored skirt may or may not fit closely around the hips. As for other skirts, 2 to 4 inches are always necessary, more if desired.

Test with a tapemeasure when measuring the necessary width at the bottom, remembering that the finer the material, the greater the fullness may be.

28
Gored Skirts

METHOD

1. Decide the number of gores.

2. Multiply the waist measurement by the number of stitches to the inch and use the nearest number of stitches that will divide by the number of gores.

3. Add the necessary number of inches to the hip measurement (according to fit desired and the width at the bottom) and multiply by the number of stitches to the inch; then use the nearest number divisible by the number of gores.

4. Multiply the width at the bottom by the stitches to the inch and use the nearest number divisible by the number of gores.

5. Divide the number of gores into the number of stitches at the waist, hips, and bottom to find the number of stitches in each gore at those points.

6. Subtract the number of stitches in each gore at the hips from the stitches in each gore at the bottom to learn the number of stitches to decrease.

7. Subtract the number of stitches in each gore at the waist from the number of stitches at the hips to learn the number to decrease.

8. Divide the number of stitches to decrease into the number of inches, first, from the bottom to the hips, second, from the hips to the waist, to learn where to decrease.

MEASUREMENTS

Waist—28 inches.
Length—31 inches minus 1 inch for crochet.
Hips—38 inches (9 inches down).
Width at the bottom—76 inches with 12 panels
or gores.

Stitch Gauge—6 stitches to the inch.

Since this gored skirt is for an average figure, we shall make it fitting from the hips to the waist and use 12 panels with 2 purled stitches between.

EXAMPLE

If the number of stitches allocated at different points does not divide evenly into the number of panels, take the nearest number that will. Follow Diagram 76.

▶ Waist—28 inches times 6 stitches to the inch = 168 stitches, 12 gores into 168 goes 14 times; therefore, each gore has 12 knit stitches with purl 2 between.

▶ Hips—a full skirt, therefore, 2 inches added to the hip measurement. 38 plus 2 inches = 40 inches, times 6 stitches to the inch is 240 stitches.

▶ There are 12 panels, therefore, 12 into 240 goes 20 times, which means that at the hip, the gores have K. 18 with P. 2 between.

▶ 3. Width at the bottom—76 inches times 6 stitches to the inch is 456. 12 into 456 stitches goes 38 times; therefore, there are K. 36 stitches in each gore with P. 2 between.

▶ From the bottom of the skirt to the hips, the knits have to be reduced from 36 to 18, that is, 18 stitches in each gore. 2 stitches are taken off at one time, so there will be 9 decreases. 9 decreases into 21 inches goes twice and 3 inches over. Therefore, there will be 3 decreases every 3 inches, and 6 decreases, 2 inches.

Always decrease by K. 1, K. 2 together at the beginning and K. 2 together, K. 1 the last 3 stitches.

▶ From the hips to the waist, we have to decrease 18 to 12, which means 6 stitches. See the diagram. Reduce 1 stitch at a time, first at one side then at the other, every inch.

▶ **PROJECTS** ◀

▶ *Using the measurements from the previous chapter, diagram and chart a 12-gored skirt with P. 2 between,*

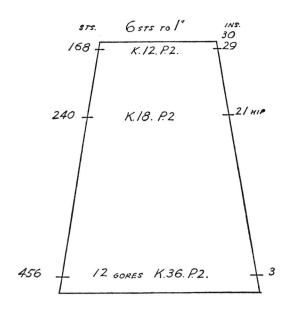

6 sts to the inch

Sts		Ins	
168		30	
168	K.12.P.2.	29	last inch even
		28	
		27	
		26	
		25	
		23	
240	K.18.P.2.	21	Hip
		19	
		17	
		15	
		13	
		11	
		9	
		6	
		3	
456	12 gores - K.36.P.2.		

DIAGRAM 76

width at the bottom—76 inches and 2 inches added at the hips. The stitch gauge—6 stitches to the inch.

▶ *Check answers on page 241.*

DIFFERENT STITCH GAUGES AND LENGTHS

In a wide gored skirt, it may be necessary to decrease more than 2 stitches in each gore at one time. In which case, knit 2 together in the center as well as at the beginning and end of each gore.

First version

MEASUREMENTS

> Waist—28 inches.
> Hips—38 inches (9 inches down) 2 extra inches added.
> Width at the bottom—80 inches, 8 gores with purl 2 between.
> Length of skirt—31 inches.
> Knitted length—30 inches.
>
>> Stitch gauge—7 stitches to the inch.

EXAMPLE

▶ Waist—28 inches times 7 stitches to the inch = 196 stitches. There are 8 gores, so 200 stitches are necessary. 8 into 200 goes 25 times, so there are K. 23 with P. 2 stitches between.

▶ Hips—a full skirt, so only 2 inches are added to the hip measurement. 38 inches plus 2 inches = 40 inches, times 7 stitches to the inch makes 280 stitches. 8 gores into 280 stitches is 35, so there are K. 33 and P. 2 between each gore.

▶ Width at the bottom—80 inches times 7 stitches to

the inch = 560 stitches. 8 gores into 560 is 70 times; therefore, K. 68 and P. 2 between for each gore. See Diagram 77.

▶ As so many stitches have to be reduced from the bottom to the hips, it is advisable to decrease 3 stitches at a time in each gore, and 1 stitch each time from the hips to the waist.

▶ The first decrease at the bottom is as follows: K. 1, K. 2 together, K. 30, K. 2 together, K. 30, K. 2 together, K. 1.

Second version

MEASUREMENTS

    Waist—28 inches.
    Hips—38 inches (9 inches down) 2 extra inches
       added.
    Width at the bottom—76 inches with 6 gores and
       P. 1 between.
    Length of Skirt—28 inches.
    Knitted Length—27 inches.

        Stitch Gauge—8 stitches to the inch.

EXAMPLE

▶ Waist—28 inches times 8 stitches to the inch = 224 stitches, to be divisible by 6, is 222 stitches. 6 into 222 goes 37 times, i.e., K. 36, P. 1.

▶ Hips—38 inches plus 2 inches = 40 inches, times 8 stitches to the inch is 320 stitches. To be divisible by 6 is 318 stitches. 6 into 318 goes 53 stitches, i.e., K. 52, P. 1.

▶ Width at the bottom—76 inches times 8 stitches to the inch = 608 stitches, 606 stitches divided by 6 is 101, i.e., K. 100, P. 1.

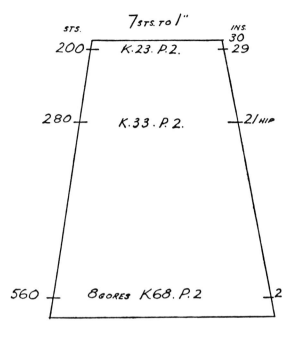

7 sts to the inch

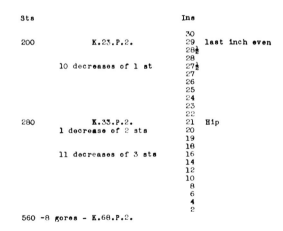

DIAGRAM 77

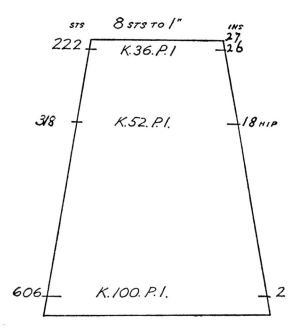

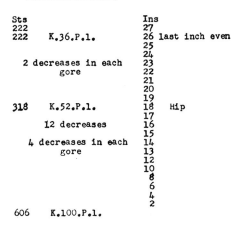

§ sts to the inch

Sts		Ins	
222		27	
222	K.36.P.1.	26	last inch even
		25	
		24	
	2 decreases in each	23	
	gore	22	
		21	
		20	
		19	
318	K.52.P.1.	18	Hip
		17	
	12 decreases	16	
		15	
	4 decreases in each	14	
	gore	13	
		12	
		10	
		8	
		6	
		4	
		2	
606	K.100.P.1.		

DIAGRAM 78

► To decrease from bottom to the hips: 100 stitches at the bottom, minus 52 stitches at the hips means 48 stitches to be reduced in each gore, i.e., 12 decreases of 4 stitches in each panel. The first decrease to be as follows: K. 1, K. 2 together, K. 30, K. 2 together, K. 30, K. 2 together, K. 30, K. 2 together, K. 1, and so on, for the others.

► To decrease from the hips to the waist: 52 stitches minus 36 stitches means 16 stitches to be reduced in each gore, i.e., 2 stitches each time (8 decreases). See Diagram 78.

► **PROJECTS** ◄

► *Using the same measurements as for the previous lesson, diagram and chart:*

An 8-gored skirt with P. 2 between, 80 inches wide at the bottom and 7 stitches to the inch, fitted at the hips.

A 6-gored skirt with P. 1 between, 76 inches wide at the bottom and 7 stitches to the inch, fitted at the hips.

► *Check answers on pages 241 to 243.*

Knitted pleated skirts are really not composed of pleats in the usual sense of the term. A number of knit and purl ribs are used; the number of stitches per inch determines the size of the ribs. The narrower the rib, the narrower the skirt appears to be.

Pleats of K. 2, P. 2, and K. 3, P. 3 are better decreased the same as flared skirts, at regular intervals. I suggest you diagram this type of skirt from the waist down, to be sure the ribs come even at the top.

There are several important factors to consider when knitting a pleated skirt:

► In a pleated or ribbed skirt, no crocheting is required; so the actual skirt length is taken into consideration when diagramming.

► In order for the entire skirt to look pleated, unlike stripes, extra material must be allowed at the hip line. This varies from at least 4 inches.

► The same applies to the waist—2 to 4 inches or more than the measurement are required.

► The number of stitches for the width at the bottom of the skirt should be 76 inches or more, depending upon

29
Pleated Skirts

the width of the rib and the type of material. The finer the material, the greater the width may be. A good criterion is that the width at the bottom should be approximately twice the hip measurement.

METHOD

▸ Multiply the width at the bottom by the number of stitches per inch. (Must be divisible by the combined knit and purl stitches of each rib.)

▸ Hips: Add the necessary allowance of at least 4 inches to the hip measurement and multiply by the stitch gauge; the number must be divisible by the total number of ribs.

▸ Waist: Add the necessary allowance to the waist measurement times the number of stitches to the inch. The number must be divisible by half the total number of ribs.

▸ Subtract the number of stitches in each rib at the hip from the stitches in each rib at the bottom to know how many to decrease—similarly from the hips to the waist.

▸ Divide the number of decreases into the inches, first, from the bottom to the hips, second, from the hips to the waist, to know where to decrease.

MEASUREMENTS

Waist—28 inches plus 2 inches is 30 inches.

Hips—38 inches plus 4 inches is 42 inches (9 inches down).

Width at the bottom—76 inches.

Length—31 inches, no allowance for crocheting.

Pleats or ribs—2 inches wide, 7 stitches to the inch, is 14 stitches.

Stitch Gauge—7 stitches to the inch.

EXAMPLE

▶ Bottom—76 inches times 7 stitches to the inch = 532 stitches. 14 knit stitches and 14 purl stitches make 28 stitches. 28 into 532 goes 19 times; therefore, there are 19 knit ribs and 19 purl ribs, making 38 ribs altogether.

▶ Hips—38 inches plus 4 inches = 42 inches times 7 stitches to the inch is 294 stitches, which must be divisible by 38 ribs. 38 does not go evenly into 294, so 304 stitches are used. 38 into 304 goes 8 times, i.e., K. 8, P. 8 at the hips. (If any number does not divide evenly, take the nearest number that will.)

▶ Waist—28 inches plus 2 inches is 30 inches times 7 stitches to the inch is 210 stitches. 19 into 210 goes 11 and 1 stitch over, so we use the number 209 stitches and have K. 6 and P. 5 at the waist.

▶ From bottom to hips—decreasing: Since there are 19 ribs, the decreasing may be 19 or 38 stitches at one time. If only the knits are decreased, the number is 19. This also applies to the purls. If both the knits and the purls are decreased, the number is 38 stitches.

▶ 14 stitches in each rib at the bottom, minus 8 stitches at the hips means 6 decreases both in the knit and purl ribs. A better-fitting skirt will result if the decreases are made gradually, first in the knits, then in the purls, allowing 12 decreases to the hips.

▶ Follow Diagram 79 for the decreases.

▶ **PROJECTS** ◀

▶ *Using the same measurements as for previous chapter, diagram and chart a pleated skirt with pleats 2 inches wide and 76 inches the width at the bottom. Stitch gauge —7 sts. to the inch.*

▶ *Check the answer on pages 243 and 244.*

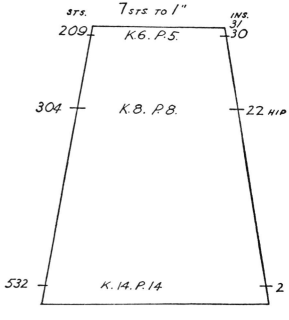

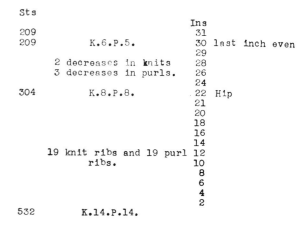

DIAGRAM 79

MACHINE-KNITTED PLEATED SKIRTS

Each pleat is knitted separately and put together afterward; therefore, too narrow ribs should not be used. These are diagrammed on the same principle as a gored skirt, decreasing on each side, and every other panel turned. So there must be an even number of panels: 14 16, 18, etc.

One must remember, too, that manufacturers' large machines are not as limited as hand-knitting machines, but the results may even be better. Generally, in cheap, pleated machine knits, the skirts are much too narrow.

All knitted garments should be thought of in terms of sewing; for in order to fit correctly there should be the same principles of clothing-construction involved.

4-GORED RIBBON KNIT SKIRT

MEASUREMENTS

- ► Waist—28 inches.
- ► Hips—38 inches plus 4 inches for straight skirt = 42 inches, 9 inches down.
- ► Width at the bottom—hip 42 inches plus 10 inches = 52 inches.
- ► Length of Skirt—30 inches, $\frac{1}{2}$ an inch for 2 rows of crocheting around the bottom, $29\frac{1}{2}$ inches for knitting.
- ► Allowance for seams—$\frac{1}{2}$ inch.
- ► Stitch gauge—5 stitches to the inch.

30

Ribbon and Machine-Knit Skirts

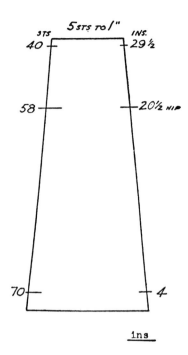

ins

last ½ inch even

8 ins x 5 is 40 sts

58 sts - 40 is
18 sts. 9 on each
side

11½ ins x 5 is 58 sts   hip

70 sts - 58 sts is
12. 6 on each side.

14 ins x 5 is 70 sts

DIAGRAM 80

EXAMPLE

4 panels are used, allowing 1 inch extra in width for each gore or panel for seams of ½ inch. See Diagram 80. For one gore, work as follows:

▶ Bottom—52 inches divided by 4 is 13 inches, plus 1 inch for seams, is 14 inches at the bottom.
▶ Hip—42 inches divided by 4 is 10½ inches, plus 1 inch for seams, is 11½ inches at the hip.
▶ Waist—28 inches divided by 4 is 7 inches, plus 1 inch for seams, is 8 inches at the waist.

MACHINE-KNIT GORED SKIRTS

The same diagramming and charting may be used for a 4-gored machine-knit skirt as for the ribbon.

A skirt with 4 or more panels or gores, and few stitches to the inch, may be decreased at the sides of each gore; but with a 6, 7, or 8 stitches-to-the-inch gauge, the decreasing should be done across the row, which is a slow process on a machine. On a slim skirt, however, the tension may be changed, using the vital measurement, the hip, to consider the necessary number of stitches.

The greater the number of gores, the better fitting the skirt, if decreasing is done at the sides.

Since it is less confusing to chart without seam allowances, I suggest you do so. Then add 4, 6, or 8 stitches to each gore for seams, according to the type of yarn.

Machine-knit 8-gored skirt

MEASUREMENTS

Waist—28 inches
Hip—38 inches

Width at Bottom—80 inches
Length—30 inches
Stitch Gauge—7 stitches to the inch
Panels—8

EXAMPLE

Waist—28 inches times 7 stitches to the inch =
196 stitches.
Hip—38 inches plus 2 inches is 40 inches × 7
stitches to the inch = 280 stitches.
Width at bottom—80 inches × 7 stitches to the
inch = 560 stitches.
Total length of skirt—30 inches minus 1 inch
for crochet.
8 panels to be used.
See Diagram 81.

In our example, the numbers are divisible by 8, but if
they do not divide, take the nearest number divisible by
the number of panels to be used. Follow the diagram.
For one gore, work as follows:

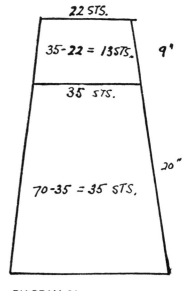

DIAGRAM 81

MEASUREMENTS

1. Waist—196 stitches divided by 8 is 24 stitches.
2. Hip—280 stitches divided by 8 is 35 stitches.
3. Bottom—560 stitches divided by 8 is 70 stitches.

EXAMPLE

4. Bottom to waist—70 stitches minus 35 stitches is 35
stitches to be decreased, decreasing on both sides 17
times, and once on one side, making 18 decreases altogether. Therefore, 2 decreases are 2 inches apart and 16
are 1 inch.

5. Hip to waist—35 stitches minus 24 stitches are 11 stitches to be decreased, 5 on one side and 6 on the other. 6 decreases in 9 inches, so the first 2 are 2 inches apart and 4 one inch apart.

6. Do not forget the seam allowances.

▶ **PROJECT** ◀

► *Diagram and chart a 4-gored ribbon- or machine-knitted skirt with the following measurements:*

> *Waist—29 inches.*
> *Hips—39 inches plus 4 inches.*
> *Width at the bottom—53 inches.*
> *Lenth of skirt—31 inches (½-inch crochet al-*
> *lowance).*
> *Knitted length—30½ inches.*
> *1-inch seam allowance for each gore.*
> *Stitch gauge—5 stitches to the inch.*

► *Check the answers on page 244.*

31
Finishing and Blocking Skirts

MEASURING LENGTH

Knitting must be stretched the necessary width before measuring length. The length, too, should be slightly stretched since the material flattens when it is steamed, as you learned when taking a stitch gauge. This applies to yarns made of wool or part wool. For special novelty yarns, and there are many on the market, use the suggestions offered in the knitting manual for that particular material. We have already considered ribbon and silk. Linen has a tendency to be weighty also; so allow for stretch of 2 or 3 inches, depending upon the amount of necessary material.

These instructions do not alter the charting of the skirt. Allow for stretch when measuring the length.

CROCHET FINISHING

A single crochet is used in knitting for finishing around many types of skirts, to complete the top, and also to flatten the edges of other knitted garments. Use a #1 steel-crochet hook for ribbon; a number 4 or 5 steel-

ILLUSTRATION 55

DIAGRAM 82

crochet hook is the best for all general purposes. All single crochet should be made fairly tight when finishing knits. If anything, the edge should be slightly drawn before steaming. Always crochet on the right side.

METHOD

► Insert the hook into the actual loop of the knit-stitch.*
► Thread over the hook and draw the thread through the stitch—2 loops on the hook.
► Thread again over the hook and draw it through both loops.*
► Repeat in each stitch.

CASING

A casing is generally used at the top of a knitted skirt, except for ribbon, to hold the elastic. This is worked inside the top of the skirt after several rows of single crochet have been made.

METHOD

► Catch the yarn at the top by means of a slip-stitch.
► Chain 4, 5, or 6 stitches, depending upon the size of the yarn, to make approximately ¾ inch.
► Fasten by means of a slip-stitch with the chain sloping diagonally (as in Diagram 82), first to the top, then to the bottom.

BLOCKING

In Chapter 13, we discussed blocking a sweater and stated the necessary equipment.

Finishing and blocking are the final steps and most

important in obtaining a beautiful knit garment. Furthermore, some mistakes can be corrected at this point.

The word, "blocking," to many, is some sort of magic trick that only a few are capable of performing. Actually, it means the pinning, steaming to shape, and flattening where necessary of a knitted or crocheted garment according to the necessary measurements of the individual; and, as I stated in Chapter 13, with the exception of ribbon-knits (which are usually finished and blocked by professionals), I definitely do not agree that every piece should be blocked separately. I have seen some sad shapes with armholes and necklines pulled, steamed, and overpressed way out of line. If the pieces are fastened together, one holds the other in shape.

Use the measurements that were taken for the finished garment according to the necessary specifications. For ribbon knits where each piece is blocked separately, you know what each should measure; or if knitting from directions from a knitting manual, break down the number of stitches to inches.

RIBBON KNITS

Turn to Chapter 13 for necessary materials.

The big difference between blocking ribbon from other materials is that ribbon garments are placed on the blocking board right side up, so that you can see that the ribbon is flattened on the right side. We shall block the panel which was previously diagrammed.

The first step is to mark the position for the gore or panel on the blocking pad. See Diagram 83.

FIRST METHOD

1. Mark the center of the panel, AB, on the board, using a long wooden rule.

2. Mark a line, CD, at right angles to AB, where the

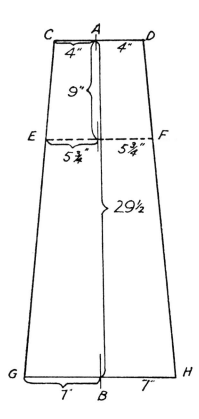

DIAGRAM 83

waist of the panel is to be pinned, using half the waist measurement on each side, which is 4 inches.

3. Measure 9 inches down AB, and mark EF, at right angles to it, using half the hip (for each panel) on each side, which is 5¾ inches.

4. On AB, measure 29½ inches which is the length of the finished skirt—29½ inches before crocheting. The other half inch is added when the skirt panels are put together.

5. Draw GH at right angles to AB, using half the width at the bottom of the panel, which is 7 inches on each side.

SECOND METHOD

1. With pins, mark the center of the actual panel on the right side.

2. Pin the center of the panel to center AB.

3. Pin the waist to CD.

4. Pin bottom to GH.

5. Pin hip to EF.

6. Pull the sides and pin in place, pins about 1 inch apart (use rule to be sure the edges are straight).

7. Press each panel as stated for ribbon stitch gauge.

8. Leave on the pad until dry.

9. Press pin marks down the center.

10. Block each panel separately.

11. Complete the skirt as in Chapter 30.

12. Press the seams and check the measurements.

FINISHING A RIBBON GORED SKIRT

METHOD

► After blocking each piece, the seams are basted and sewn, allowing one-half inch seams. This may be done on a machine with a loose, fairly long stitch, being sure the rows match at the seams, or by hand with a back stitch. Leave an opening at the left side for a zipper 5 to 7 inches long: Ribbon does not stretch like wool or other yarns.

➤ Work 2 rows of single-crochet around the lower edge of the skirt and one around the upper, on the right side.

➤ Sew in the zipper, leaving half-inch allowance at the top.

➤ Single crochet around the zipper on the right side to hide it.

➤ Cut the stiffened belting to the waist measurement, allowing an extra 1½ inches for the turn backs for closing, on which the hooks and eyes are fastened.

➤ Baste and sew the belting, then the hooks and eyes.

LINING RIBBON KNITS

I do not advocate lining a ribbon knit made of rayon or rayon and silk ribbon, if a fairly close pattern stitch has been used. The beauty of all knits is their flexibility. If a tight lining is added, their charm is lost; and they become much too hot and heavy for comfort.

If rayon, silk, or nylon ribbons are used in a very loosely knitted, crocheted, or hairpin-lace stitch, they need a foundation. For a slim sheath, a satin foundation may be made the exact size and fastened loosely at the seams by means of catch stitches; or for lighter wear, nylon net or tulle may be used.

You know the measurements of your finished garment; or, if you desire, baste and block your garment, then take the pattern from the pieces, allowing half-inch seams.

Sew the seams, catch stitch them to the garment, then hem around the neckline, bottom, and zipper.

I reiterate, one must know dress design to become an expert knit designer.

SKIRTS MADE ON A CIRCULAR NEEDLE

For skirts which are made partly of ribbon, e.g. ribbon stripes, and using a circular needle, I would advise that the ribbon stripes be partly pressed before being blocked like a yarn skirt. The principle for pinning skirts made on a circular needle is very much the same as blocking a panel, except that skirts knitted of materials other than ribbon are all turned on the wrong side to block and are completely finished before any steaming takes place.

For a dress, it is better to block the skirt and top separately, if possible. At any rate, the skirt should be completed, that is, the casing for the elastic worked or the belting sewn in.

We shall take for our example the measurements of the skirt diagrammed in Chapter 25. Remember, we block to the finished measurements.

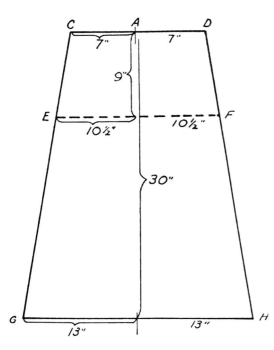

DIAGRAM 84

MEASUREMENTS

> Waist—28 inches.
> Hip—42 inches (9 inches down).
> Width at the bottom—52 inches.
> Length—30 inches.

Follow Diagram 84 and mark the measurements on the blocking pad, just as for the panel.

EXAMPLE

► Place the pins down the center front and the center back of the skirt, dividing it in two.

► Half the waist, 28 inches, is 14 inches; therefore, 7 inches on each side of the center.

► Half of the finished hip, 42 inches, is 21 inches; therefore, 10½ inches on each side of center front (9 inches down).

► Half of the width at the bottom, 52 inches, is 26 inches, 13 inches each side of the center.

► Pin the center front and the center back together down the center line, AB.

► Complete the pinning as for the panel.
► Steam as for the sweater, Chapter 13, Steps 14 to 17.

▶ **PROJECTS** ◀

► *Test your ability on a skirt.*

TRADITIONAL SLACKS

Use medium weight yarn—12 to 16 ounces. Take the measurement from a pair of well-fitting slacks and figure accordingly. Slacks are made in four pieces, right and left sides, making the back length of the crotch 1 inch longer. See Illustration 56.

MEASUREMENTS

Waist—28 inches.
Length of crotch—14 inches (back); 13 inches (front).
Length of leg—25 inches.
Stitch gauge— 8 stitches to the inch.
12 rows to the inch.

EXAMPLE

1. One-quarter of the waist is 7 inches. 7 $\times$ 8 stitches to the inch is 56 stitches.

32
Women's Slacks and Bikinis

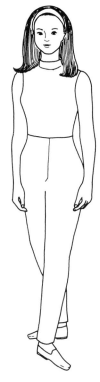

ILLUSTRATION 56

2. Crotch back: increase every ninth row (¾ inch), 16 times—12 inches.

3. Side front: at the same time, increase every ninth row (¾ inch) 12 times, 9 inches. 3 inches even—84 stitches.

4. Continue working even at the side, and at the crotch 1 inch even, then add 2, 2, 3, 4, 5, and 8 stitches, every other row, at the crotch side, making 108 stitches.

5. Decrease every ½ inch, 30 times (crotch side), and every 1¼ inches (side), 20 times, making 58 stitches.

6. Decrease 10 times, every 12 rows or 1 inch, at the crotch side, and even at the side, for 10 inches, making 15 inches—25 inches total for the leg.

7. Work 4 pieces in all, allowing a 7- or 9-inch zipper at the left side and complete as for sweaters in Chapter 13, and top of skirts.

SHORTS

Figure as for slacks, making the legs the desired width and length according to figure.

BELL-BOTTOMS

Here, too, 4 pieces are used. Use the actual waist measurement, although 2 inches below the waist at the top. This will make the slacks fit tightly and stay in position. Make 4 pieces exactly the same, using 7 inches down for hips. Use stockinette stitch. See Illustration 57.

MEASUREMENTS

Back 1 inch longer in crotch.

Total length—39 inches
12 inches to crotch

25 inches leg
26 inches waist
36 inches hips

Stitch Gauge— 8 stitches to 1 inch.
10 rows to inch.

EXAMPLE

► Starting at the top: one quarter of waist is 6½ inches x 8 stitches to the inch is 52 stitches.

► One-quarter of 36 inches for hip is 9 inches x 8 stitches to inch is 72 stitches.

► 72 stitches less 52 stitches is 20 stitches, 10 stitches at each side. Increase at both sides, every ½ inch, 10 times, and 7 inches down, or 84 rows.

► Knit 3½ inches even, until stitches added at one side for crotch, but no increasing at side seam.

► Add 2 stitches, every second row, then 4 stitches for crotch, making 88 stitches. See diagram.

► Decrease 1 stitch every ½ inch, at both sides, 20 times. 48 stitches remain, and 10 inches for leg.

► Work 5 inches even, now 15 inches for leg.

► Increase at both sides, every half inch, 20 times, making 88 stitches, and leg 25 inches long.

► Slip stitch pieces together as for sweaters, allowing a 9 inch zipper at the left side.

BIKINIS

Bottom

I suggest using medium weight yarn, wool, and a size smaller needle than that generally used for that type of material. I also suggest ribbing, since it has a tendency

ILLUSTRATION 57

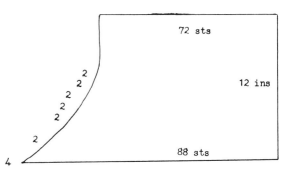

DIAGRAM 85

to tighten rather than stretch when wet and, therefore, not feel cold when out of the water.

Materials to be used are:
        2 ounces of medium weight yarn;
        Size 1 straight needles.—Knit tightly.

MEASUREMENTS

Width:
        32 inches—16 inches (back), 16 inches (front).
        K.2, P.2 ribbing

Stitch gauge:
        7 stitches to the inch.
        10 rows to the inch.

EXAMPLE

Start at the front and make in one piece, all K.2, P.2

➤ 32 inches x 7 stitches to the inch is 224 stitches. ½ of 224 stitches is 112 stitches.
        ➤ For 3 inches—stretch when measuring.
        ➤ Decrease 2 stitches at the beginning of every row until 36 stitches remain. Approximately 4 inches, making 7 inches.
        ➤ Work 2 inches even.
        ➤ Increase 2 stitches at the beginning of every row until 112 stitches.
        ➤ Rib 4 inches even, making 17 inches—stretch when measuring.
        ➤ Bind off.
        ➤ Sew side seams, easing the 3 inches of front into 4 inches of back.
        ➤ If desired make beading for elastic inside top as for skirts.

ILLUSTRATION 58

Tops

Round cup.   Use medium weight yarn, wool, 1 ounce, and set of 4 #12 needles.

MEASUREMENTS

>Circumference 16 inches but divisible by 4.
>Stitch Gauge— 7 stitches to inch
>10 rows to inch

EXAMPLE

▶ 16 inches x 7 stitches to the inch is 112 stitches. Use 108 stitches, 36 stitches on each of 3 needles.

▶ Use ribbing of K.2.P.2, knitted tightly for 2 inches.

▶ Decreasing:

K.2 stitches, P.2 stitches together for 1 round, leaving a ribbing of K.2.P.1., which is worked for 1 inch.

K.2 stitches together, P.1. for 1 round, leaving ribbing of K.1.P.1. which is worked for ½ inch.

K.1.P.3 stitches together, for one round, leaving ribbing of K.1.P.1. which is worked for ½ inch.

K.2 together all the way around.

Draw remaining stitches together using darning needle, fasten tightly.

▶ Single crochet around millinery elastic, using #5 steel crochet hook. This will give body around outside.

▶ Knit identical second piece, and complete as #1.

▶ Attach tape or cord as in illustration.

Triangular cup.   Use 1-oz. medium weight yarn, with size 1 straight needles.

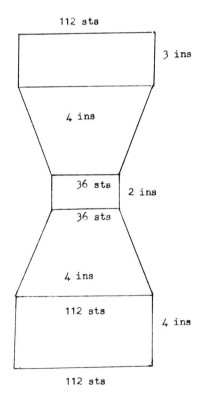

DIAGRAM 86

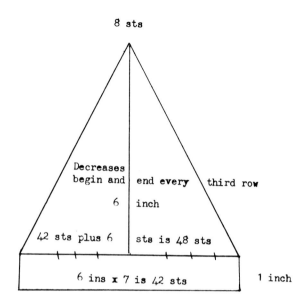

8 sts

Decreases begin and | end **every** \ third row
6 | inch
42 sts plus 6 | sts is 48 sts
6 ins **x** 7 is 42 sts   1 inch

DIAGRAM 87

MEASUREMENTS

Stitch Gauge— 7 stitches to the inch
10 rows to the inch
Knit tightly using stockinette stitch.

EXAMPLE

▶ Begin with a 6 inch width. 7 stitches to inch × 6 is 42 stitches. Stockinette stitch 1 inch even.

▶ Increase in every 7th stitch, 6 times, making 48 stitches.

▶ Knit 2 together at the beginning and end of every 3rd row, 20 times, which is 40 stitches reduced and 6 inches in length, 8 stitches left.

▶ Bind off the 8 stitches tightly.

▶ Single crochet around millinery elastic, using #5 steel crochet hook. This will tighten to form cup and also give body around outside.

▶ Knit 2 identical pieces; attach as in illustration, and fasten 4 pieces of tape or cord, 15 inches long.

33
Children's
Knitted Wear

Since age is the poorest predictor of children's body measurements—because many children of the same age have entirely different body proportions—we are fortunate that we have mastered the taking of measurements for all sizes and are able to adjust the measurements to suit the style, material, and need of the child.

I do want to offer a word of caution, however; do not add an inch here and an inch there to allow for growth. Let us consider an upper-arm measurement of 9½ inches that was made 10½ inches, then 2 inches more added for the width of a sleeve as for an adult, instead of the necessary 1½ inches for a child. This would be large enough for a medium-sized woman.

There are three essentials for children's garments:

► Ease in dressing: simple design.
► A size large enough to take into consideration rapid growth.
► Suitable color.

Since we know how to lengthen and shorten all necessary parts, let us make them correctly in the first place and have a happy, contented, comfortable child.

There follows a chart of measurements which might be valuable to those who instruct in knit shops, designers, or those who wish to make sweaters, etc., of a specific size.

These measurements are the finished measurements after the article has been steamed or blocked.

SIZES	2	3	4	6	8	10	12	14
Chest	23	24	25	26½	28	29½	31	33
Underarm to waist (includes rib)	8	9	10	10½	11	11½	12½	13
Upper arm	9	10	10½	11	11	11½	12	12½
Armhole (around)	10	10½	11	12	13	14	15	16
Underarm sleeve	8	9	10	11	12	13	14½	16
Shoulder-to-shoulder	10½	11	11½	12	12½	13	13½	14

It is not necessary to decrease at the hips of a skirt for a child. Decrease straight from the bottom to the waist.

For sizes 1, 2, 3, and 4, I think it advisable to add all the necessary stitches for the width of a sleeve on the first row after the ribbing. A fitted sleeve is not always practical unless one is making a small coat sleeve; then don't make that too fitted.

▶ *PROJECTS* ◀

▶ *Diagram and chart the following skirts:*

Plain stockinette
  Waist—24 inches
  Length—19 inches
  Width—48 inches
  Stitch gauge—6 stitches to the inch

Pleated: same measurements as above
  Bottom—52 inches
  Pleats—3 inches wide

▶ *Check measurements on pages 245 and 246.*

NECESSARY QUALIFICATIONS FOR SUCCESS

"I've been knitting since I was six. Many have asked me to teach them to knit, so I think I'll open a knit shop."

How little is understood of the attributes necessary to operate a successful business!

Knitting has developed into high fashion (apart from knitting mittens, socks, hats, etc.) and entails a knowledge of knit design, color, and alterations, as well as merchandising, advertising, personality traits, and business acumen, which can only be gained through learning, understanding, and experience.

Skill

Skill in giving instructions and directions to the customer does not simply mean that one should be able to knit and purl adequately, or even be able to follow instructions from a knitting manual. One must have a thorough knowl-

34
Operating
a Knit Shop

edge of knit design and be able to change any instruction to suit individual needs and wants, as well as be able to diagram and chart every possible garment, ranging from sweaters to evening gowns, for any type of figure. Every skill, therefore, comes into play, including finishing, blocking, and lining, if necessary.

Knowledge of merchandise

Some of the most difficult materials to know in the U.S.A. and Canada are the different yarns, threads, ribbons, etc., from which knitted garments are made. We have already spoken of some of the more common yarns, but there are literally hundreds of different types and brands sold by different distributors and manufacturers, from many countries of the world. My suggestion is to spend as much time as possible in large art needlework departments—different stores will carry different brands because of their franchises—or, better still, become proficient in diagramming and charting and gain experience as an instructor. There is no better way of learning the potentialities of different yarns.

One must know how to buy yarn and needles intelligently. An adequate stock of each should be kept on hand; and I suggest some no-dye-lot yarns for general use, especially for beginners. Do not be afraid to stock a staple brand because a large department store carries the same. Your personality and courtesy to customers will soon overcome the difference in size between your shop and the large store, for yours is one business where automation cannot take over. It is important, also, to know the correct amount of yarn to sell to a customer for her requirements. The amounts cannot be given here, for there are so many yarns; but my suggestion is to refer to the knitting manual which is using a given brand for a similar type of garment. Finally, be careful not to undersell yarns with a dye number.

Knowledge of fashion trends

Knits are the closest to four-season apparel and wearable any time of day. They also pack well, travel well, and shed wrinkles.

To keep up with fashion trends, I suggest you subscribe to and digest the material in the leading women's magazines, *Harpers Bazaar, Vogue, Glamor, Seventeen, Cosmopolitan,* etc. One garners inspirations not only from knits! Good styling is learned in subtle ways, from many sources. Note color trends, but do not become an addict to fashionable colors: Most importantly, colors must be suitable to the individual's needs. See the section in this chapter on color.

For the sake of reference, I suggest you keep files.

Habits

You must maintain a satisfactory level of performance at all times and have a systematic, scientific method that others may follow. In other words, if a sales person or instructor is employed, you train, teach, and encourage her in your method of proficiency. The sale of merchandise is really your end result; and the reputation of your business depends upon how well your customers are satisfied with their finished product.

Advertising

I suggest you try leaflets from door to door, or a newspaper advertisement with a special attraction for the opening. The inducement need not be too elaborate—perhaps a small give-away token, a tapemeasure with the shop's address. With knitting taking the lead in women's hobbies, the news of the opening will soon circulate.

For your displays, ask for photo releases, mat and copy services from your manufacturers. Try to obtain or make one or two models with quick selling appeal. To ascertain the maximum percentage of gain, make sure to study the costs of materials.

To my mind, there are no better forms of advertising than word-of-mouth news from a satisfied customer and your own appearance when you are offering your merchandise. The correct styling, color, and material of your own garments will help establish a good customer relationship: What if you are on the heavy side? Your customer may be, too. It is a fallacy to think that knits should only be worn by the very slim: Knitted skirts, like sewn skirts, will neither "cup" nor creep up at the knee if enough room is allowed for spread.

Business acumen

You must have the ability to shoulder responsibilities:

Stand behind your merchandise and your instructions at all times.

You should know how to buy the right merchandise at the right time and be able to keep adequate records, write a business letter, and figure discounts and interests. Maintaining adequate records is extremely important and may provide the key to your success or failure.

Keep daily record sheets from the cash register; and record cash and credit sales, layaways, purchases for both customers and yourself, wages, rent, utilities, incidentals, etc.

And, until you are established, be willing to do a variety of tasks and to work long hours.

Your chances for success

I think it will be realized that not everyone has the qualifications to operate a business successfully, but today there is ample opportunity for anyone who has ability in this area.

Having read the previous paragraphs, you should take stock of your personal assets and rate yourself on your qualifications. Throughout my many years as teacher and author, I have always considered that nothing is impossible if one makes up one's mind to succeed. True, about one-third of small businesses fail the first year and approximately one-sixth in the second; but if you honestly feel you can and will succeed, here are a few suggestions.

How to begin

I have had many students who first started in a small way in their own homes, made a success of it, then branched out into a shop.

Find a shop in a suitable location with a not-too-high rental and, if possible, near a shopping center that brings pedestrian traffic near your doors. Ask your local Chamber of Commerce for suggestions.

When outfitting and furnishing the shop, remember that proper lighting is most important for helping customers and displaying merchandise.

Your basic equipment should include a sales counter, showcases, tables, comfortable chairs, a cash register, plus all the necessary equipment for finishing and blocking garments.

In terms of stock, manufacturers' representatives will be of help to you. Don't overload with too many brands or types of yarns. It is much better to have a sufficient supply of one type so that a customer is not kept waiting. Be careful not to overstock with slow-moving numbers that are apt to tie up too much capital. The amount of stock to be carried depends, too, upon the shopkeeper's proximity to her source of supply.

The following are good sources of information: Trade

publications such as *Notion and Novelty Review, Gift and Art Buyer, Merchants Trade Journal* and the art needlework and craft publications.

The U.S. Government Department of Commerce has informative booklets for helping small businesses. Write to Supt. of Documents, U.S. Government Printing Office, Washington, D.C.

Vocations in the knitting field

One of the greatest needs of our country today is the finding of some form of industry that is not governed by automation. Hand-knitting is one of these. There is a great need for experts in this line, since knitting, because of its relaxing qualities, is fast becoming the leading hobby of women in America.

The following are a few possible vocations:

► Teaching in adult education classes, recreation departments, the Y.W.C.A., and rehabilitation centers.

► Instructing in shops.

► Designing.

► Repairing and restyling hand- and machine-knit garments.

► Writing newspaper and magazine articles and directions for knitting manuals.

► Chapter 18 is my *Complete Book of Progressive Knitting* gives more information on vocations that are available.

I cannot stress too much, however, that in any of these positions one should have a thorough knowledge of the principles outlined in *Knit to Fit.*

COLOR

Today nearly every woman knows the value of charm, so we must be on the alert to find an irresistible color when we are considering any form of dress design.

I want to stress that one should never choose a color because it happens to be in vogue for that particular season. We must also remember that as we grow older, the pigmentation of skin, eyes, and hair change. Those with tinted hair must be particularly careful. Close to the face, subdued colors are especially essential so as not to call attention to the inevitable lines.

A good idea is to have a range of your own colors—pieces of material large enough to drape around the upper part of the bust and throat, of different textures, if possible. Texture can alter the effect that a color produces: A vivid color may look harsh in a hard-surfaced fabric, but if the fabric has depth, it may become vibrant and flattering. Choose a piece of material comparable to the material you wish to use, depending upon the purpose, the occasion, the season, and the need (for example, traveling).

One of the important elements neglected in many knit shops is the importance of color: Prestige would be gained if there were more emphasis on color. Industry has taken advantage of the vast new potential of color. Exciting, uncommon colors have been created by the yarn manufacturers. To keep a customer, one must be able to provide complete satisfaction after the garment has been tried and tested. Be sure though, that you have sufficient quantity of material of a given color in stock. Having to wait two or three weeks for material would dampen the ardor of any customer.

Color values

Red. Red is exhilarating, recently having blossomed forth in all its glory, alone or in combination. And, it is fashionable for any season of the year. Since it is rich, warm, and aggressive, red is really more suitable for cooler seasons. Older women with good figures may look well in some shades of red but should be wary of wearing too bright a color or wearing it too close to the face:

Something soft in material and subdued in color might be more pleasing. Instead, try adding a scarf of pink. Shades of pink have an air of festivity, and the right shade can be worn by almost anyone.

Blue.   Blue gives a sense of relaxation. There are cool and serene grayed-blues, and warm and exotic ones, but pick the tones that *accentuate* rather than *diminish* your own coloring. Some blues may be so strong that they detract from the color of your eyes and make them appear wishy-washy.

Green.   Green may be refreshing and cool, but beware of yellow-green if your complexion is sallow.

Yellow.   Yellow with its many shades from yellow-beige to orange is used a great deal and can give a sense of well-being.

Gray.   Gray is neutral.

Purple.   Purple is dramatic.

Black and White.   Black and white are in a category apart. Those with fading color and graying hair should remember that black absorbs light and tends to drain color from the face. White reflects heat and so is considered the coolest color.

Finally, ask yourself these questions: Is the color suitable for your figure proportions? Should you wear one solid color or should some subtle trickery be used to hide some figure discrepancies?

Black or grayed colors tend to make the figure appear smaller and slimmer than do bright and light colors.

A bright panel from neck to hem makes the wearer look taller.

One who wishes to appear shorter may use a two-tone effect, broken across the figure.

To minimize the waist, use a band of cool color or change the width of the belt.

A large bust can be minimized by the use of diagonal lines or by wearing dark or cool colors on the top portion of garment, and bright colors at the bottom.

▶ *PROJECT* ◀

Since choosing the correct colors is a very important phase of knit design, study colored fashion illustrations from magazines and books and consider why they attract you. Notice the colors that are chosen for a particular type of person and the style of the garment.

Features governing selection of colors to suit individual needs

Complexion, hair, and eye colors are so interrelated that they must all be considered when selecting colors.

An important consideration is whether the color makes you look more pale, more sallow, or rosier: Remember that the lower the natural pigmentation, the softer, less-accented the color should be. All skins are black, yellow, or pink in varying degrees. If yellow is the predominating hue the skin is considered warm-toned, so wear colors that blend with yellow—shades from red-orange to yellow, red-browns, rose-beiges and golden-yellows. When pink predominates, the skin is pink-toned and cool in appearance and, therefore, needs no highlighting. Soft, muted colors should be worn.

Among hair colors, white is the coolest. Black comes next, because it has no warmth. The third in coolness is light ash-blond. Golden blonds are definitely warm; whereas redheads, ranging from light golden-red to auburn, are in the warm category.

Eyes are also classified as warm or cool. The brown group are considered warm, hazel eyes warm-to-cool (according to whether the brown flecks predominate), and all the blues and grays are cool.

The physical type of the light, or true, blond applies to

those whose complexion ranges from very fair to golden tones, hair light to golden blond, and eyes light-blue to brown. This person may wear colors that are clear and fresh-looking—blues, purples, greens, and any pastels. Black, too, may be stunning. If the coloring is very delicate, however, be sure it is not overpowered with vivid colors. Emphasize this delicacy; it is an asset.

A medium blond usually has a medium complexion, hair between blond and light-brown, and eyes that run the gamut from blue to brown. The same categories of colors can be worn as the light-blonds, but they should not be as vivid, since they would detract from the neutral, natural coloring of the hair and skin.

The person with true red or auburn may have a very fair skin, or the complexion may be as dark as a brunette's, with blue, gray, hazel, or dark-brown eyes. Blues, greens, and attractive browns are good. Reds, pinks, deep purples are considered taboo for all but the most daring. But whether white or yellow predominates in the skin tones, the auburn-haired person has distinctive coloring that should be made the most of.

Similarly, a brunette of the "Irish type"—white skin, blue or blue-gray eyes, and dark hair—is extremely attractive because of the striking contrasts.

A medium brunette may have hair which is chestnut or brown, eyes blue to brown, and skin fair to olive. Since this is the most predominant "type" in America, pay special attention to details that raise her out of the general run. She should use very distinctive colors that are definitely not drab to add a touch of the exotic to her appearance.

A dark brunette's skin may be vary fair to black, hair brown to black, and eyes varying from blue-gray to black. She may wear true colors in most instances, but if she has a sallow complexion, a too extreme yellow-green or orange will emphasize her sallow skin.

Sometimes, in the case of gray-haired women, when

natural pigmentation leaves the skin, it may develop a clear almost cameo quality. Soft and subtle colors and white emphasize this ethereal look. If your hair is steel-gray or pure white, with few exceptions, you may follow the dictates of your eyes and skin colors. But if your hair is streaked with yellowish or brownish wisps, be careful not to emphasize these. Avoid yellow, brown, and tan. And above all, one should dress according to one's age.

▶ *PROJECT* ◀

Read articles on color, charm, and personality. Have files for light blonds, medium blonds, medium brunette, dark brunette, and gray.

ALTERATIONS

For one who desires to earn a livelihood in a special line of work, alteration and finishing could become a very lucrative business. Besides, anyone who handles hand-knits, designs herself, instructs, or knits for others, should know how to alter garments without ravelling them completely.

As we have seen in the chapter on straight skirts, it is advisable to start all hand-knit skirts at the bottom. The correct tension of the stitch, the stitch gauge, is assured by the time the important fitting areas (namely the hips and the waist) are reached.

One must realize that it is impossible to ravel any knitting or crocheting from the beginning. No knitting or crocheting can be pulled out backwards.

Shortening a hand-knitted skirt

If the skirt "cups," or "sits out" at the back, it may be lifted and the extra length taken from the top. But if the skirt fits satisfactorily, shorten in the following way.

METHOD

▶ Mark the desired length of the skirt, which, no matter what fashion dictates (mini, midi, or maxi), should meet individual needs.

▶ Break a thread just above this length, as though snagging a stocking.

▶ Pull out the thread as far as possible, before it breaks. The knit loops will remain facing downward and will not pull out.

▶ Using a #4 or #5 steel crochet hook slip-stitch (crochet) in all the loops. (#4 or #5 crochet hook is all right for all general purposes and much faster than using a knitting needle.)

▶ Continue to pull out the yarn and slip-stitch in the loops until they are all secured.

▶ Single crochet around the bottom several times to prevent the skirt from rolling.

Lengthening a hand-knitted skirt

The following can only be done with stockinette stitch. The joining shows if one breaks a thread in ribbing.

METHOD

▶ Break a thread near the bottom of the skirt, about 3 rows up.

▶ Pick up the stitches on the same number circular needle that was used to knit the skirt, or a smaller size, then knit on the correct size. Pick up the stitches from the back so the loops will not be twisted.

▶ Knit for the desired length.

▶ Single crochet around the bottom several times and

always on the right side, in each stitch and just a little tighter than the knitting.

Altering sweaters

To shorten or lengthen sleeves, break a thread above the ribbing, at the necessary place to lengthen or shorten the sleeve, then knit down, adding the ribbing.

To lengthen a sweater from underarm to waist, follow the steps given below.

METHOD

► Undo the side seams for several inches above the ribbing.

► Break a thread about 3 rows above the ribbing, either at the front or back.

► Knit down the desired length, using the used yarn.

► Decrease instead of increase at the waist for the ribbing.

► Knit the other half to correspond and slip-stitch the seams.

Remodeling machine-knitted garments

It is impossible to unravel machine-knitted dresses and sweaters that are cut to shape.

METHOD

► After the garment has been fitted and the correct position of the seams and hem marked, machine-stitch several times just inside the cutting line, so that the material will not ravel.

► Cut and sew on a machine, just like a woven fabric.

► If any part has to be shortened, single crochet just as for a hand-knit.

▶ *PROJECT* ◀

Make a small piece of fabric of stockinette stitch. Break a thread and lengthen one inch.

PRICES

I want to add prices for alterations, finishing, and blocking. Of course, these prices vary with the store, the nature of the material, the clientele, the section of the country, and prevailing salaries.

Sweaters

► The flat rate for completely finishing sweaters—$5.50 to $8.00.
► Finishing the neck with either ribbing or collar—$1.00 to $3.00.
► Seams—$2.50 to $4.00.
► Ribbon down the front and finishing buttonholes—$1.50 to $3.50.
► Finishing buttonholes without ribbon—25 to 35 cents each.
► Hand-crocheted buttons—25 to 35 cents each.
► Blocking—$2.00 to $4.00.

Finishers should receive 50 to 80% of the price. Do not skimp on this cost: The work of the finisher is extremely important, takes considerable time, and deserves adequate compensation.

If the sweater has been charted correctly and knitted according to instructions, it will only be necessary to steam and flatten the seams. I feel that, if sweaters did not cost so much for finishing and upkeep, women would be more enthusiastic about making other garments.

Dresses

For finishing and blocking dresses, use the following as a guide.

Woolen Dresses—$15.00 to $25.00
Yarn and Ribbon—$35.00 to $50.00
Ribbon—$50.00 to $65.00

For blocking and cleaning dresses, the prices are in the following ranges.

Yarn—$4.50 to $ 6.00
Ribbon—$7.00 to $10.00

Suits may cost a little more, depending upon the style.

Washing knits is preferable to dry cleaning. Many call this "wet blocking." It simply means that the garment is pinned on the board immediately after washing.

Shortie coats

For finishing, lining, and blocking shortie coats, use the following guide.

Finishing—$10.00 to $12.50
Lining—$10.00 to $12.50
Blocking—$ 4.00 to $ 6.50

Machine knits

Alterations for machine knits are in the following price ranges.

Shortening the bottom of a skirt—$ 4.50 to $ 6.50
Making a 2-piece from a 1-piece—$15.00 to $16.50
Lengthening skirts—$12.50 to $15.00

Made-to-order dresses

The prices of dresses hand-knit "from scratch" and sold in exclusive stores are as follows.

Wool and novelty yarns—$225.00 and up
Ribbon—$400.00 and up

Knitters

If you employ knitters, there is quite a difference in prices —for average-weight yarn, $1.75 to $2.50 a ball is a fair price. In some localities, knitters are paid by the yard, 1 to 1½ cents. For ribbon knits, $65.00 and up, depending upon the style of the garment. Of course, all the finishing has to be done afterwards.

Mark-up for trade

Figure your cost—that is the material and the labor—then mark-up 50%. That is the wholesale price. The 50% allows for your overhead. Then if you sell to the trade, their mark-up is 50% more than they paid to you. Do not forget the 2% discount allowed for 10 days, etc.; and make sure what each buyer means by "10 days." I have known the time to be manipulated to about two months.

Answers

CHAPTER 2

Page 9

► You should have no difficulty with the garter stitch. Remember not to cast on stitches with a larger needle, or the bottom loops will be too loose.

► Does there seem to be a difference in the look of rows in your stockinette stitch? It is more than possible that you are purling looser than you knit. Tighten tension.

► Many women knit ribbing loosely. Be especially cognizant of this fact and watch your tension. Does the second stitch of your K. 2, P. 2 look larger? Increase the tension when changing stitches.

► Always decrease at the very edge, not one stitch in, and watch out not to have apparent holes in your increasing. You may have placed your needle in between the stitches, not directly in a stitch.

► Did you bind off loosely? Is the edge elastic? When binding off for shaping that is hidden in a seam, it is permissible to bind off with knit stitches; but, for ribbing, moss stitch, etc., always bind off as you would if you were working the next row. Did you bind off your ribbing correctly?

CHAPTER 6

Page 41

The diagram and chart to the armhole of the back of the man's slipover and cardigan: See Diagrams 88 and 89.

$\frac{1}{2}$ Waist—19 inches
$\frac{1}{2}$ Chest—21 inches
Waist-to-underarm—11 inches
$\frac{1}{2}$ Armscye—10$\frac{1}{2}$ inches
Shoulder-to-shoulder—17 inches
Stitch gauge—6 stitches to the inch

1. 19 inches x 6 stitches to the inch = 114 stitches for the ribbing.
2. 21 inches x 6 stitches to the inch = 126 stitches for the body.
3. 126 stitches minus 114 stitches leaves 12 stitches.
4. 12 into 114 stitches is 9$\frac{1}{2}$; therefore, increase first in the 9th stitch, then in the 10th stitch on the first row after the ribbing.

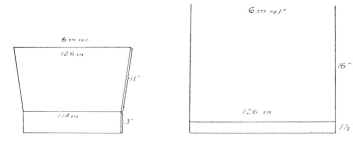

DIAGRAM 88   DIAGRAM 89

The diagram and chart to the armhole of the back of the woman's slipover and cardigan: See Diagrams 90 and 91.

> ½ Waist—14 inches
> ½ Bust—18 inches
> Waist-to-underarm—8 inches
> ½ Armscye—9½ inches
> Shoulder-to-Shoulder—14½ inches
> Stitch gauge—7 stitches to the inch

1. 14 inches x 7 stitches to the inch = 98 stitches for the ribbing.

2. 18 inches x 7 stitches to the inch = 126 stitches for the body.

3. 126 stitches minus 98 stitches leaves 28 stitches.

4. 28 into 98 stitches is 3½; therefore, increase first in the 3rd stitch, then in the 4th stitch on the first row after the ribbing.

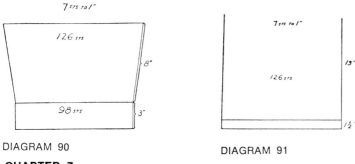

DIAGRAM 90

DIAGRAM 91

CHAPTER 7

Page 47

Four steps in shaping armholes for a man's sweater:

1. Shoulder-to-shoulder measurement is 17 inches x 6 stitches to the inch = 102 stitches.

2. ½ chest measurement is 126 stitches minus shoulder stitches, 102, leaves 24 stitches to take off at both armholes (12 at each).

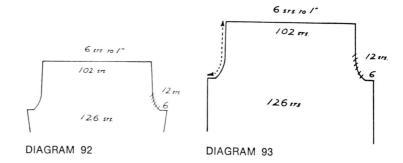

DIAGRAM 92   DIAGRAM 93

3. Bind off 6 stitches at the beginning of the next 2 rows, then knit 2 together at the beginning and end of the next 6 knitted rows.

4. Knit even to ½ the armhole measurement, 10½ inches, measuring around. See Diagrams 92 and 93.

Four steps in shaping armholes for a woman's sweater:

1. Shoulder-to-shoulder measurement is 14½ inches x 7 stitches to the inch = 102 stitches.

2. ½ bust measurement, 126 stitches minus shoulder stitches, 102, is 24 stitches to take off at both armholes, 12 at each.

3. Bind off 6 stitches at the beginning of the next 2 rows, then knit 2 together at the beginning and end of the next 6 knitted (front) rows.

4. Knit even to ½ the armhole measurement, 9½ inches, measuring around. See Diagrams 94 and 95.

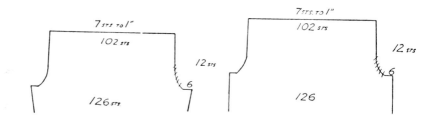

DIAGRAM 94   DIAGRAM 95

Stitches for shoulder—102 stitches.

Stitch gauge—6 stitches to the inch, 4 slopes.

1. A slipover sweater with an opening, with shoulders for round, oval, square, or V-necklines (Diagram 96).

2. A slipover sweater without an opening, with shoulders for high-round and turtle-necklines (Diagram 97).

3. A cardigan of general styling (Diagram 98).

Diagrams and charts for shoulders of women's sweaters:

Stitches for shoulder—102 stitches.

Stitch gauge—7 stitches to the inch, 5 slopes.

1. A slipover sweater with opening, with shoulders for round, square, oval, or V-necklines (Diagram 99)..

2. A slipover sweater without an opening, with shoulders for high, round, and turtle-necklines: (Diagram 100).

3. For a cardigan of general styling (Diagram 101).

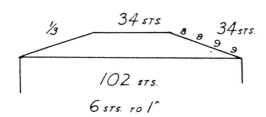

DIAGRAM 96

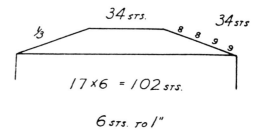

DIAGRAM 97

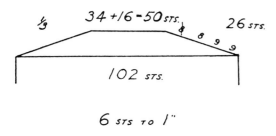

DIAGRAM 98

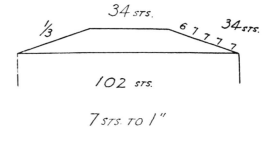

DIAGRAM 99

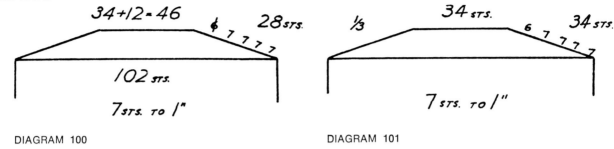

DIAGRAM 100

DIAGRAM 101

DIAGRAM 102

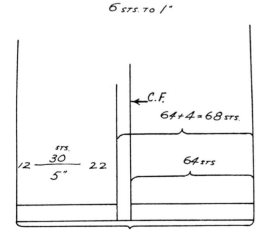

CHAPTER 9

Page 59

Place the position of pockets on the fronts of cardigans as follows. For a man:

1. Total back—126 stitches.
2. ½ of 126 stitches is 63, even number, 64 stitches.
3. ½ width of band is 4 stitches plus 64 stitches is 68 stitches.

For the pocket:

1. 5 inches = 30 stitches, at 6 stitches to the inch.
2. 64 minus 30 stitches leaves 34 stitches.
3. ⅔ of 34 stitches is 22 stitches to the center front.
4. ⅓ is 12 stitches to the side seam (Diagram 102).

For a woman:

1. Total back—126 stitches.
2. Half of 126 stitches is 63, even number, 64 stitches.
3. Half width of band is 4 stitches plus 64 stitches = 68 stitches.

For the pocket:

1. 4 inches = 28 stitches, at 7 stitches to the inch.
2. Two-thirds of 36 stitches is 24 stitches to the center front.

3. One-third is 12 stitches to the side seam (Diagram 103).

CHAPTER 10

Page 63

A man's high, round neckline with opening (slipover):

► 102 stitches for shoulders. Knit half way, 51 stitches. 51 stitches minus 34 stitches for the shoulder leaves 17 stitches.

► Bind off 9 stitches the first row, then knit 2 together, every front row, 8 times.

► If armhole is not the same as the back, knit even until the same length (Diagram 104).

A man's high, round neckline without opening (slipover). (Do not work the last slope of the shoulder at the back):

► 102 stitches for the shoulders. Knit half way, 51 stitches minus 26 stitches for shoulder = 25 stitches.

► Bind off 13 stitches the first row, then knit 2 together, every front row, 12 times (Diagram 105).

A man's high round neckline for cardigan:

► 56 stitches minus half the width of the band, 4 stitches = 52 stitches to the center front.

► 52 stitches minus shoulder stitches, 34, leaves 18 stitches. Bind off 9 stitches and 2 together, 9 times, but—

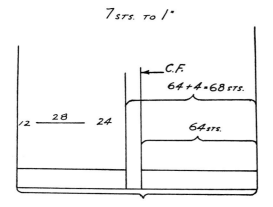

DIAGRAM 103

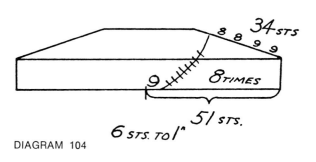

DIAGRAM 104

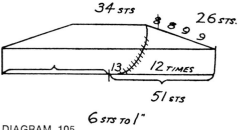

DIAGRAM 105

▶ Add half the width of the band, 4 stitches, to the first bind off, 9 plus 4 = 13 stitches (Diagram 106).

A woman's neckline with opening (slipover):

▶ 102 stitches for shoulder. Knit half way, 51 stitches. 51 minus 34 stitches for shoulder = 17 stitches.

▶ Bind off 9 stitches the first row, then knit 2 together, every front row, 8 times.

▶ If the armhole is not the same length as the back, knit even until the same length (Diagram 107).

A woman's neckline without opening (slipover):

▶ Do not work the last slope of the shoulder at the back.

▶ 102 stitches for shoulders. Knit half way, 51 stitches. 51 stitches minus 28 stitches for the shoulder leaves 23 stitches.

▶ Bind off 12 stitches the first row, then knit 2 together, every front row, 11 times (Diagram 108).

A woman's neckline for cardigan:

▶ 56 stitches minus half the width of the band, 4 stitches, is 52 stitches to the center front.

▶ 52 stitches minus shoulder stitches, 34, leaves 18 stitches. Bind off 9 stitches and knit 2 together, 9 times, but—

▶ Add half the width of the band, 4 stitches, to the first bind off, 9 plus 4 = 13 stitches (Diagram 109).

A woman's V-neckline:
The diagrams are self-explanatory.

1. 2 inches after the first bind off at the armhole, or when all the armhole stitches have been decreased, knit 2 together, every front row (Diagram 110).

2. At the first bind off at the armhole, knit 2 together, every fourth row, i.e., every second front row (Diagram 111).

3. Just above the waistline, knit 2 together, every 8th row, i.e., every 4th front row (Diagram 112).

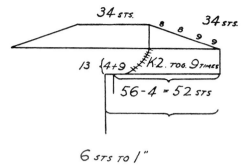

34 STS.   34 STS.

8 8
9 9

13 {4+9   K.2. TOG. 9 TIMES

56 − 4 = 52 STS

6 STS TO 1"

DIAGRAM 106

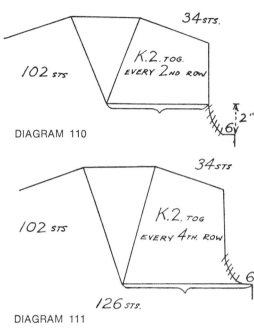

34 STS.

102 STS   K.2. TOG.
EVERY 2ND ROW

6   2"

DIAGRAM 110

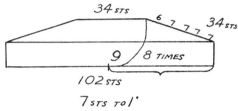

34 STS

6 7 7 7 7
34 STS

9   8 TIMES

102 STS

7 STS TO 1"

DIAGRAM 107

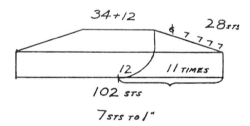

34 + 12

28 STS
6 7 7 7 7

12   11 TIMES

102 STS

7 STS TO 1"

DIAGRAM 108

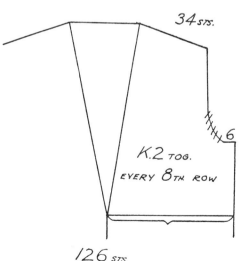

34 STS

102 STS   K.2. TOG
EVERY 4TH. ROW

6

126 STS.

DIAGRAM 111

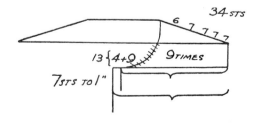

34 STS

6 7 7 7 7

13 {4+9   9 TIMES

7 STS TO 1"

DIAGRAM 109

34 STS.

6

K.2. TOG.
EVERY 8TH. ROW

126 STS.

DIAGRAM 112

CHAPTER 11

Page 71

A man's long sleeves (see Diagram 113).

> Wrist—8 inches
> Upper arm—13 inches
> Sleeve length—20 inches
> Stitch gauge—6 stitches to the inch

1. Wrist—8 inches plus 1 inch = 9 inches. 9 inches x 6 = 54 stitches. Add 2 stitches for K. 2, P. 2, making 56 stitches.

2. 2 inches added to the first row after the ribbing is 56 stitches plus 12 stitches, which = 68 stitches.

3. Upper arm is 13 inches plus 3 inches = 16 inches x 6 stitches to the inch = 96 stitches.

4. 96 stitches minus 68 stitches leaves 28 stitches to be increased—14 stitches at each side.

5. Increase 1 stitch at the beginning and end of row, every inch, 14 times.

For the cap:

1. Bind off 6 stitches at the beginning of next 2 rows, then knit 2 together at the beginning and end of each front row, until 4½ inches of stitches—28 stitches—remain; then bind off 2 stitches, until 2 inches, 12 stitches are left.

2. Bind off.

A woman's long sleeve (See Diagram 114).

> Wrist—6 inches
> Upper arm—11 inches
> Sleeve length—17½ inches
> Stitch gauge—7 stitches to the inch

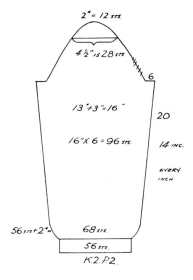

DIAGRAM 113

1. Wrist—6 inches plus 1 inch = 7 inches. 7 x 7 stitches to the inch = 49 stitches, even number, 50 stitches.

2. 1 inch added to the first row after the ribbing, 58 stitches.

3. Upper arm is 11 inches plus 2 inches = 13 inches x 7 stitches to the inch = 91 stitches, even number—92 stitches.

4. 92 stitches minus 58 stitches = 34 stitches, 17 stitches at each side.

5. Increase 1 stitch at the beginning and end of row, every three-quarter inch, 17 times.

6. Knit even until underarm measurement is reached.

For the cap:

1. Bind off 6 stitches at the beginning of the next 2 rows; then knit 2 together at the beginning and end of each front row, until 3½ inches of stitches, 26 stitches, remain; then bind off 2 stitches until 2 inches, 14 stitches, are left.

2. Bind off.

A cap straight out from the shoulder (Diagram 115).

Shoulder-to-shoulder—15 inches
Half bust measurement—18 inches
Cap—3 inches
Stitch gauge—7 stitches to the inch, 10 rows to the inch

1. 18 inches x 7 stitches to the inch = 126 stitches.

2. 15 inches x 7 stitches to the inch = 104 stitches for the shoulders.

3. 126 stitches minus 104 stitches is 22 stitches to take off for armscyes, 11 stitches for each.

4. 3-inch cap is 21 stitches.

5. 21 stitches minus 11 stitches leaves 10 stitches to add at the underarm, 1 stitch, every other row, 3 times, then 7 stitches all at one time.

A cap slightly fitting at the upper arm (Diagram 116).

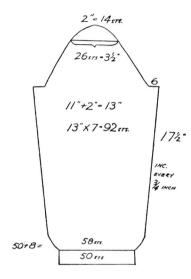

DIAGRAM 114

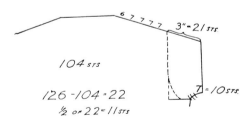

DIAGRAM 115

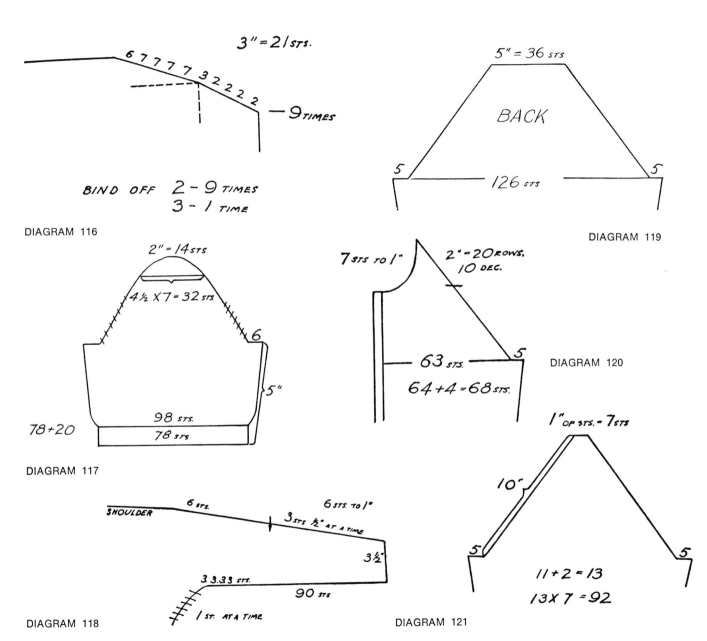

$3'' = 21$ STS.

6 7 7 7 7 3 2 2 2 2

— 9 TIMES

BIND OFF 2 - 9 TIMES
3 - 1 TIME

DIAGRAM 116

$5'' = 36$ STS

BACK

5   126 STS   5

DIAGRAM 119

$2'' = 14$ STS

$4½ × 7 = 32$ STS

6

5"

78 + 20

98 STS.
78 STS

DIAGRAM 117

7 STS TO 1"

$2'' = 20$ ROWS,
10 DEC.

63 STS.
$64 + 4 = 68$ STS.

5

DIAGRAM 120

SHOULDER 6 STS.

6 STS TO 1"
3 STS ½" AT A TIME

3½"

3 3.33 STS.
1 ST. AT A TIME

90 STS

DIAGRAM 118

$1''$ OF STS. - 7 STS

10"

5   5

$11 + 2 = 13$
$13 × 7 = 92$

DIAGRAM 121

1. Bind off 2 stitches, every other row, 9 times, and 3 stitches once, making 20 rows.

2. 20 rows at 10 rows to an inch = 2 inches.

3. This is 2 inches less than half required width of straight cap, or half the armhole measurement.

For a short sleeve, Diagram 117 is self-explanatory.
For a long dolman sleeve, see Diagram 118.

Underarm to waist—8 inches minus 3 inches leaves 5 inches.
Sleeve underarm length—18 inches minus 3 inches leaves 15 inches.
Shoulder stitches the same as for set-in sleeve.
Stitch gauge—6 stitches to the inch.

1. Add 1 inch of stitches, 1 stitch at a time, every other row, at the underarm, i.e., 6 stitches.

2. Add 2 inches of stitches, half an inch at a time, i.e., 3 stitches, every other row.

3. 15 inches x 6 stitches to the inch = 90 stitches to add all at one time.

4. Knit even the desired half width of the cuff, 3½ inches.

5. Bind off half an inch of stitches, 3 stitches, every other row, for half the length of the sleeve, 7½ inches, = 45 stitches.

6. Bind off 1 inch of stitches, 6 stitches, until the shoulder stitches remain.

7. Shape the shoulder.

For raglans with set-in sleeves, Diagrams 119, 120, 121 are self-explanatory.

CHAPTER 14

Page 95

For a man's sweater with set-in sleeves:

Half waist—19 inches
Half chest—21 inches
Shoulder-to-shoulder—17 inches
½ armhole—10½ inches
Stitch gauge—6 stitches to the inch

Diagram 122 is self-explanatory.

For a man's sleeveless sweater, follow Diagram 123, which shows necessary changes.

For a woman's sweater with set-in sleeves:

Half waist—14 inches
Half bust—18 inches
Waist-to-underarm—8 inches
Shoulder-to-shoulder—14½ inches
Half armhole—9½ inches
Stitch gauge—7 stitches to the inch

Diagram 124 is self-explanatory.

Diagram 125 for a sleeveless sweater shows the necessary changes.

For a sleeveless sweater with 5 cables, the cables are to be evenly spaced, using P. 2, K. 6, P. 2 (Diagram 126):

Half waist—19 inches
Underarm-to-waist—11 inches

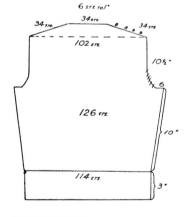

DIAGRAM 122

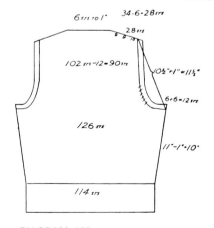

DIAGRAM 123

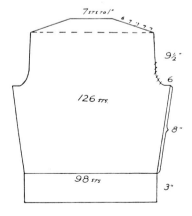

DIAGRAM 124

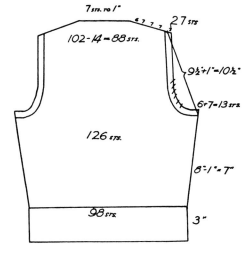

DIAGRAM 125

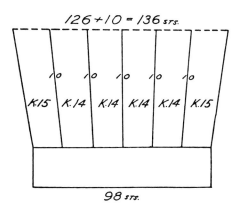

DIAGRAM 126

Half chest—21 inches

Stitch gauge—6 stitches to the inch

1. 126 stitches plus 10 stitches for 5 cables = 136 stitches

2. 5 cables using 10 stitches each = 50 stitches

3. 136 stitches minus 50 stitches = 86 stitches for 6 spaces; therefore, K. 14 for 4 spaces, and K. 15 for each end.

CHAPTER 15

Page 99

For a woman's weskit with square neckline:

> Half waist—14 inches
> Half bust—18 inches
> Waist-to-underarm—8 inches
> Shoulder-to-shoulder—14 inches
> Half armhole—9½ inches
> Stitch gauge—7 stitches to the inch

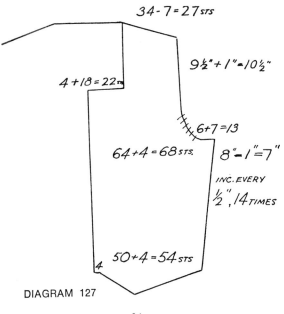

34-7=27 STS

9½"+1"=10½"

4+18=22 STS

6+7=13

64+4=68 STS.   8"-1"=7"

INC. EVERY
½", 14 TIMES

50+4=54 STS

4

DIAGRAM 127

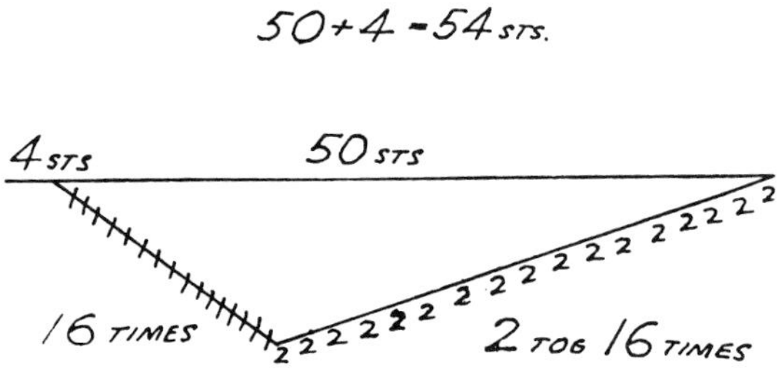

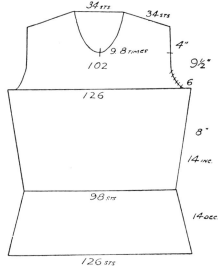

34 STS   34 STS

9. 8 TIMES   4"

102   9½"

126   6

98 STS   8"

14 INC.

98 STS   14 DEC.

126 STS

DIAGRAM 129

50+4=54 STS.

4 STS   50 STS

16 TIMES   2 TOG 16 TIMES

DIAGRAM 128

If you have understood the other lessons, Diagrams 127 and 128 are self-explanatory.

CHAPTER 16

Page 103

For a woman's fitted sweater with oval neckline (Diagram 129):

Half waist—14 inches
Half bust—18 inches
Waist-to-underarm—8 inches
Half armhole—9½ inches
Hip, 6 inches below waist—36 inches
Stitch gauge—7 stitches to the inch

1. 126 stitches minus 98 stitches leaves 28 stitches. 14 stitches to decrease at each side, in 6 inches—a little less than every half inch.

2. Similarly, 14 stitches to be increased on each side, every half inch, 2 inches even to the underarm.

3. Neckline—Oval neckline starts 4 inches below the tip of the shoulder.

9½ inches minus 4 inches leaves 5½ inches; therefore, at 5½ inches, decrease for oval neckline, which is the same as a low, round neckline. 34 stitches from 51 stitches leaves 17 stitches. Bind off 9 stitches and knit 2 together, 8 times.

CHAPTER 17

Page 107

For a wide, off-shoulder, scoop neckline for evening sweater and blouses (Diagrams 130 and 131):

Shoulder-to-Shoulder—15 inches
Neckline—6 inches deep at the center and ends, 2 inches below the tip of the shoulder
Stitch Gauge—7 stitches to the inch, 10 rows to the inch

   1. 15 inches x 7 stitches to the inch = 105 stitches, use 104 stitches. ½ of 104 is 52 stitches to the center.
   2. 6 inches minus 2 inches to the tip of the shoulder leaves 4 inches in which to decrease 52 stitches.
   3. 10 rows to the inch x 4 = 40 rows, or 20 rows on which to bind off.
   4. 20 into 52 goes twice and 12 stitches over; therefore, bind off 3 stitches at the neck edge, 12 times, and 2 stitches, 8 times.

   For a wide, on-shoulder oval neckline (Diagrams 132 and 133):
   The measurements are the same as those given for the off-shoulder scoop neckline.
   The neckline starts 5 inches below the tip of the shoulder and uses 2 shoulder slopes.

   1. 15 inches x 7 stitches to the inch = 105 stitches, use 104 stitches. Half of 104 is 52 stitches to the center, 7 stitches to the inch, therefore 5 shoulder slopes.
   2. Depth of neckline 5 inches x 10 rows to the inch = 50 rows, or 25 rows on which to decrease at the front edge.
   3. 52 stitches minus 14 shoulder stitches leaves 38 stitches to be decreased in 25 rows. Use 1 row for the first bind off, therefore, 38 minus 24 = 14 stitches to be

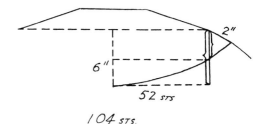

DIAGRAM 130

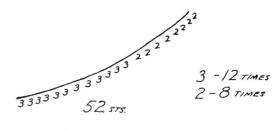

DIAGRAM 131

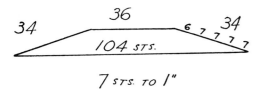

34   36   6 7 7 7 34
104 sts.

7 sts. to 1"

DIAGRAM 132

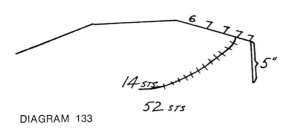

6 7 7 7
5"
14 sts.
52 sts

DIAGRAM 133

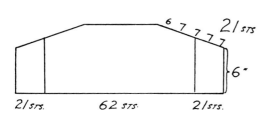

6 7 7 7   21 sts
6"
21 sts.   62 sts.   21 sts.

DIAGRAM 134

bound off at the beginning, then knit 2 together, at the front edge, every other row, 24 times.

4. Bind off the 2 shoulder slopes.

A wide, square on-shoulder neckline starts 6 inches below the tip of the shoulder and uses 3 shoulder slopes.

1. 3 shoulder slopes = 21 stitches, therefore 42 stitches for both.

2. 104 stitches minus 42 stitches leaves 62 stitches for the neckline.

3. Knit 21 stitches. Bind off 62 stitches.

4. Knit even on remaining 21 stitches until the shoulder is reached.

5. Shape the shoulder.

6. Knit the other side, reversing the shaping (Diagram 134).

CHAPTER 22

Page 133

Differences in measurements between sweaters and blouses.

	SWEATER	JACKET	
Waist	28 inches	plus 2 inches	= 30 inches
Across back	17½ "	plus 1 inch	= 18½ "
Front bust	18½ "	plus 1 inch	= 19½ "
Underarm-to-waist	8 "	minus ½ inch	= 7½ "
Shoulder-to-shoulder	14½ "	plus 1 inch	= 15½ "
Sleeve underarm length	17½ "	minus ½ inch	= 17 "
Wrist	6 "	same	
Upper arm	11 "	same	
Armscye	19 "	plus 1 inch	= 20 inches

For the back of fitted jackets—darts:

Half waist—15 inches

Across back underarm—20 inches

Across front bust—22 inches

Shoulder-to-shoulder—15½ inches

Underarm-to-waist—8 inches
Waist to hip—17½ inches, 5 inches down
Stitch gauge—7 stitches to the inch

1. Hips—17½ inches x 7 stitches to the inch = 124 stitches

2. Waist—15 inches x 7 stitches to the inch = 104 stitches

3. Across back underarm—20 inches x 7 stitches to the inch = 140 stitches

4. Shoulder-to-shoulder—15½ inches x 7 stitches to the inch = 108 stitches

5. Decreases and increases:

> Bottom to waist—124 stitches minus 104 stitches leaves 20 stitches, 10 stitches at each side to decrease every ½ inch.
>
> Waist-to-underarm—140 stitches minus 104 stitches leaves 36 stitches. Increase 8 stitches in each dart, 2 stitches at a time, every 1½ inches; 4 times, making 16 stitches; and 10 times, every ¾ inch at the sides for a total of 36 stitches. See Diagram 135.
>
> Underarm-to-shoulder—15½ inches x 7 = 108 stitches. 140 stitches minus 108 stitches leaves 32 stitches, 16 at each side.

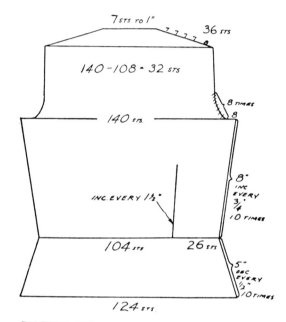

DIAGRAM 135

For the front of fitted jackets—darts:

The sides are shaped in the same way as the back, and there are the same number of shoulder stitches.

Across front bust—22 inches; half is 11 inches x 7 stitches to the inch or 77 stitches (78 even number).

Note that no allowance has been made for overlap in front.

Follow Diagram 136:

1. 78 stitches minus 52 stitches leaves 26 stitches. 10 decreases and 10 increases at the side to match the back shaping; therefore, 16 stitches to be increased in a dart.

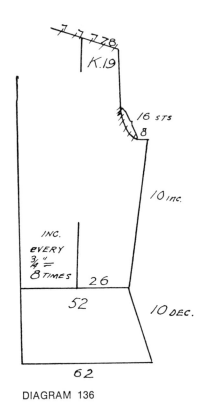

DIAGRAM 136

2. Place a marker at half the waist, 26 stitches, then increase before and after the marker, every ¾ inch, 8 times, as follows: Knit 24 stitches, increase in a stitch, K. 1, marker, K. 1, increase in a stitch, and so on.

3. Shoulder dart—As 18 stitches is the center of the shoulder, and 8 stitches have to be decreased in a dart, begin 5 inches below the tip of the shoulder, and decrease every inch, 4 times, as follows: K. 19, K. 2 together, K. 1, marker, K. 1, K. 2 together.

CHAPTER 23

Page 139

For the box coat:

> Across the back underarm—22 inches
> Front bust—12 inches for each front
> Armscye—20 inches
> Shoulder-to-shoulder—15½ inches
> Length from underarm—14 inches
> Sleeve—14 inches
> Stitch gauge—7 stitches to the inch

For the back:

1. 22 inches x 7 stitches to the inch = 154 stitches for 14 inches.

2. As 2 inches in width were added across the back, the 2 inches of stitches is reduced in darts at the shoulders. See Diagram 137.

3. Bind off 8 stitches at the armscye, then knit 2 together, 7 times, so 16 stitches remain for the darts, 8 for each shoulder.

For the front:

1. 12 inches x 7 stitches to the inch = 84 stitches plus 6 stitches for the overlap = 90 stitches. Knit even for 14 inches.

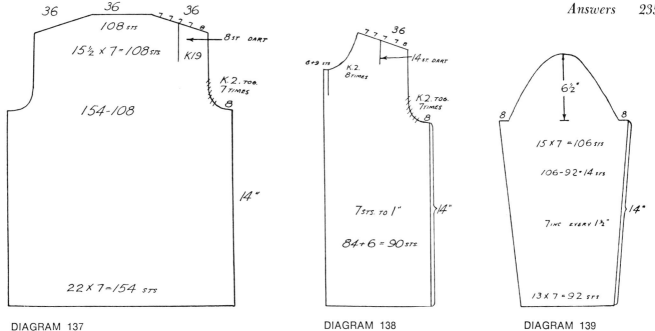

DIAGRAM 137

DIAGRAM 138

DIAGRAM 139

2. Armscye same as the back.

3. 2 inches taken off in dart, 14 stitches, 2 at a time, starting 6 inches from the tip of the shoulder, every ¾ of an inch. See Diagrams 137 and 138.

For the sleeve, Diagram 139 is self-explanatory.

CHAPTER 26

Page 153

Do the following exercises for straight skirts (Diagram 140):

Waist—29 inches
Hips—39 inches (9 inches below the waist)
Length—31 inches, minus 1 inch for crochet leaves 30 inches knitted length

Stitch gauge—6 stitches to the inch

1. Waist is 29 inches x 6 stitches to the inch = 174 stitches, nearest 10, 170 stitches.

2. 39 inches plus 4 inches = 43 inches x 6 stitches to the inch = 258 stitches, nearest 10, 260 stitches.

3. Width at the bottom is 43 inches plus 10 inches = 53 inches x 6 stitches to the inch = 318 stitches, nearest 10, 320 stitches.

4. Decreases

Bottom to hips—320 stitches minus 260 stitches leaves 60 stitches or 6 decreases of 10 stitches each.

15 inches to the hips—6 into 15 inches goes 2 and 3 inches over; therefore, there are 3 decreases of 3 inches and 3 decreases of 2 inches. Hips to waist—260 stitches minus 170 stitches leaves 90 stitches or 9 decreases of 10 stitches each.

For straight skirts with different stitch gauges use the same measurements as those in Chapter 26.

Stitch Gauge—7 stitches to the inch.

1. Waist—29 inches x 7 stitches to the inch = 203 stitches, nearest 10, 200 stitches.

2. Hips—39 inches plus 4 inches = 43 inches x 7 stitches to the inch or 301 stitches, nearest 10, 300 stitches.

3. Width at the bottom—43 inches plus 10 inches = 53 inches x 7 stitches to the inch or 371 stitches, nearest 10, 370 stitches.

4. Decreases

Bottom-to-hips—370 stitches minus 300 stitches leaves 70 stitches or 7 decreases of 10 stitches. Hips-to-waist—300 stitches minus 200 stitches leaves 100 stitches or 10 decreases of 10 stitches. See Diagram 141.

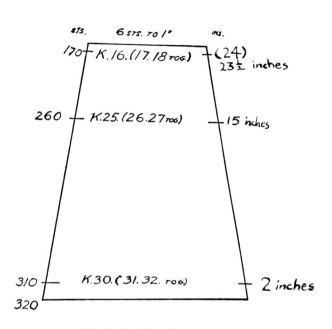

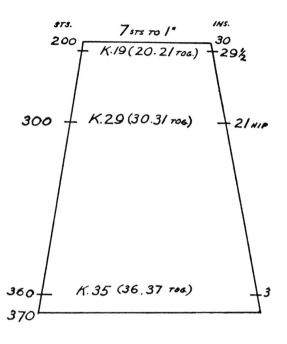

6 sts to the inch

Sts		Ins	
170		24	
170	K.16 (17.18 tog.)	23½	last ½ inch **even**
180	K.17 (18.19 tog.)	23	
190	K.18 (19.20 tog.)	22	
200	K.19 (20.21 tog.)	21	
210	K.20 (21.22 tog.)	20	
220	K.21 (22.23 tog.)	19	
230	K.22 (23.24 tog.)	18	
240	K.23 (24.25 tog.)	17	
250	K.24 (25.26 tog.)	16	
260	K.25 (26.27 tog.)	15	Hip
270	K.26 (27.28 tog.)	13	
280	K.27 (28.29 tog.)	11	
290	K.28 (29.30 tog.)	9	
300	K.29 (30.31 tog.)	6	
310	K.30 (31.32 tog.)	3	
320			

DIAGRAM 140

7 sts to the inch

Sts		Ins	
200		30	
200	K.19 (20.21 tog.)	29½	last ½ inch **even**
210	K.20 (21.22 tog.)	29	
220	K.21 (22.23 tog.)	28½	
230	K.22 (23.24 tog.)	28	
240	K.23 (24.25 tog.)	27	
250	K.24 (25.26 tog.)	26	
260	K.25 (26.27 tog.)	25	
270	K.26 (27.28 tog.)	24	
280	K.27 (28.29 tog.)	23	
290	K.28 (29.30 tog.)	22	
300	K.29 (30.31 tog.)	21	Hip
310	K.30 (31.32 tog.)	18	
320	K.31 (32.33 tog.)	15	
330	K.32 (33.34 tog.)	12	
340	K.33 (34.35 tog.)	9	
350	K.34 (35.36 tog.)	6	
360	K.35 (36.37 tog.)	3	
370			

DIAGRAM 141

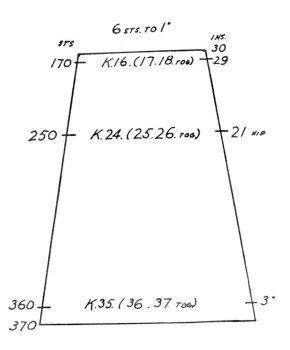

6 sts to the inch

Sts		Ins
170		30
170	K.16 (17.18 tog.)	29 last inch even
180	K.17 (18.19 tog.(	28
190	K.18 (19.20 tog.)	27
200	K.19 (20.21 tog.)	26
210	K.20 (21.22 tog.)	25
220	K.21 (22.23 tog.)	24
230	K.22 (23.24 tog.)	23
240	K.23 (24.25 tog.)	22
250	K.24 (25.26 tog.)	21 Hip
260	K.12 (13.14 tog.)	18
280	K.13 (14.15 tog.)	15
300	K.14 (15.16 tog.)	12
320	K.15 (16.17 tog.)	9
340	K.16 (17.18 tog.)	6
360	K.35 (36.37 tog.)	3
370		

DIAGRAM 142

CHAPTER 27

Page 161

For flared skirts, the measurements are the same as those in Chapter 26, allowing 1 inch for crochet in length.

Width at the bottom—61 inches; 20 inches more than the necessary hip measurement of 39 plus 2 inches, or 41 inches.

Stitch gauge—6 stitches to the inch

1. Waist—29 inches x 6 stitches to the inch = 174 stitches, use 170 stitches.

2. Hips—39 inches plus 2 inches = 41 inches x 6 stitches to the inch = 246 stitches, use 250 stitches.

3. Width at the bottom—61 inches x 6 stitches to the inch is 366 stitches, use 370 stitches.

4. Decreases

Bottom to hips—370 stitches minus 250 stitches leaves 120 stitches. Cannot divide 370 evenly by 20, so decrease 10 stitches first, then 5 decreases of 20 stitches, and 1 decrease of 10 stitches. See Diagram 142.

Hips to waist—250 stitches minus 170 stitches leaves 80 stitches, or 8 decreases of 10 stitches.

For flared skirts with different stitch gauges, use the following measurements:

Waist—29 inches
Hips—39 inches plus 4 inches = 43 inches
Length—31 inches, 1 inch for crochet = 30 inches
Width at the bottom—58 inches
Stitch gauge—7 stitches to the inch

1. Waist—29 inches x 7 stitches to the inch = 203 stitches, use 200 stitches.

2. Hips—39 inches plus 4 inches = 43 inches x 7 = 301 stitches, use 300 stitches.

3. Width at the bottom—43 inches plus 15 inches = 58 inches x 7 = 406 stitches, use 410 stitches.

4. Decreases

Bottom to hips—410 stitches minus 300 stitches leaves 110 stitches to decrease. 5 decreases of 20 stitches and 1 decrease of 10 stitches.

Hips to waist—300 stitches minus 200 stitches = 100 stitches or 10 decreases of 10 stitches. See Diagram 143.

Use the same measurements as in the previous exercise, but stitch gauge—8 stitches to the inch.

1. Waist—29 inches x 8 stitches to the inch = 232 stitches, use 230 stitches.

2. Hips—39 inches plus 4 inches = 43 inches x 8 or 344 stitches, use 340 stitches.

3. Width at the bottom—53 inches x 8 = 424, use 420 stitches.

4. Decreases

Bottom to hips—420 stitches minus 340 leaves 80 stitches or 8 decreases of 10 stitches.

Hips to waist—340 stitches minus 230 stitches leaves 110 stitches, 11 decreases of 10 stitches, or 5 decreases of 20 stitches and 1 decrease of 10 stitches. See Diagram 144.

Waist—29 inches
Hips—39 inches plus 2 inches = 41 inches
Width at the bottom—61 inches
Stitch gauge—8 stitches to the inch

1. Waist—29 inches x 8 stitches to the inch = 232 stitches, use 230 stitches.

2. Hips—39 inches plus 2 inches = 41 inches x 8 is 328 stitches, use 330 stitches.

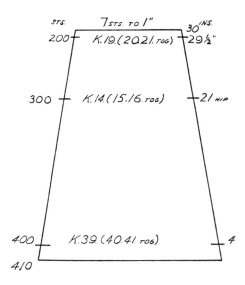

7 sts to the inch

Sts		Ins	
200		30	
200	K.19 (20.21 tog.)	29½	last ½ inch even
210	K.20 (21.22 tog.)	29	
220	K.21 (22.23 tog.)	28½	
230	K.22 (23.24 tog.)	28	
240	K.23 (24.25 tog.)	27	
250	K.24 (25.26 tog.)	26	
260	K.25 (26.27 tog.)	25	
270	K.26 (27.28 tog.)	24	
280	K.27 (28.29 tog.)	23	
290	K.28 (29.30 tog.)	22	
300	K.14 (15.16 tog.)	21	Hip
320	K.15 (16.17 tog.)	18	
340	K.16 (17.18 tog.)	15	
360	K.17 (18.19 tog.)	12	
380	K.18 (19.20 tog.)	8	
400	K.39 (40.41 tog.)	4	
410			

DIAGRAM 143

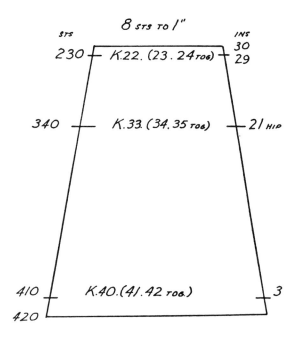

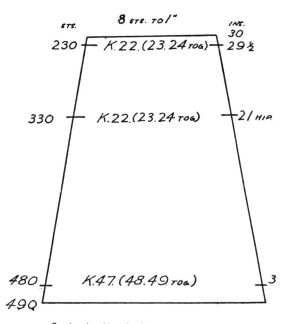

8 sts to the inch

Sts		Ins	
230		30	
230	K.22 (23.24 tog.)	29	last inch even
240	K.11.(12.13 tog.)	28	
260	K.12.(13.14 tog.)	27	
280	K.13 (14.15 tog.)	26	
300	K.14 (15.16 tog.)	25	
320	K.15 (16.17 tog.)	23	
340	K.33 (34.35 tog.)	21	Hip
350	K.34 (35.36 tog.)	19	
360	K.35 (36.37 tog.)	17	
370	K.36 (37.38 tog.)	15	
380	K.37 (38.39 tog.)	12	
390	K.38 (39.40 tog.)	9	
400	K.39 (40.41 tog.)	6	
410	K.40 (41.42 tog.)	3	
420			

DIAGRAM 144

8 sts to the inch

Sts		Ins	
230		30	
230	K.22 (23.24 tog.)	29½	last ½ inch
240		29	even
250		28½	
260	1 fewer st between	28	
270	each decrease	27	
280		26	
290		25	
300		24	
310		23	
320		22	
330	K.32 (33.34 tog.)	21	Hip
340	K.16 (17.18 tog.)	19	
360	K.17 (18.19 tog.)	17	
380	K.18 (19.20 tog.)	15	
400	K.19 (20.21 tog.)	13	
420	K.20 (21.22 tog.)	11	
440	K.21 (22.23 tog.)	9	
460	K.22 (23.24 tog.)	6	
480	K.47 (48.49 tog.)	3	
490			

DIAGRAM 145

3. Bottom—41 inches plus 20 = 61 inches x 8 = 488 stitches, use 490 stitches.

4. Decreases

    Bottom to hips—490 stitches minus 330 stitches leaves 160 stitches. 7 decreases of 20 stitches, and 2 decreases of 10 stitches.

    Hips to waist—330 stitches minus 230 stitches leaves 100 stitches or 10 decreases of 10 stitches each. See Diagram 145.

CHAPTER 28

Page 167

For a 12-gored skirt with P. 2, between:

    Waist—29 inches
    Hips—39 inches plus 2 inches = 41 inches
    Length—31 inches (30 inches knitted length)
    Width at the bottom—76 inches
    Stitch gauge—6 stitches to the inch

1. Waist—29 inches x 6 stitches to the inch = 174 stitches—nearest number divisible by 12 is 180 stitches. 12 into 180 = 15 stitches, i.e., K. 13, P. .2.

2. Hips—39 inches plus 2 inches = 41 inches x 6 stitches to the inch makes 246 stitches, divisible by 12 = 252 stitches. 12 into 252 goes 21 times, i.e., K. 19, P. 2.

3. Width at the bottom—76 inches x 6 stitches to the inch = 456 stitches, divisible by 12 is 38 stitches, i.e., K. 36, P. 2.

4. Decreases in each panel or gore

    Bottom to hips—36 minus 19 leaves 17 stitches to be decreased in each panel, 2 stitches 8 times and 1 stitch once. See Diagram 146.

    Hips to waist—19 stitches minus 13 stitches leaves 6 stitches to be decreased in each panel, 6 times.

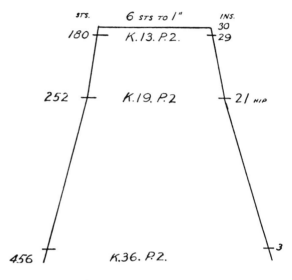

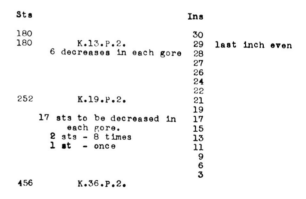

6 sts to the inch

Sts		Ins	
180		30	
180	K.13.P.2.	29	last inch even
	6 decreases in each gore	28	
		27	
		26	
		24	
		22	
252	K.19.P.2.	21	
		19	
	17 sts to be decreased in	17	
	each gore.	15	
	2 sts - 8 times	13	
	1 st - once	11	
		9	
		6	
		3	
456	K.36.P.2.		

DIAGRAM 146

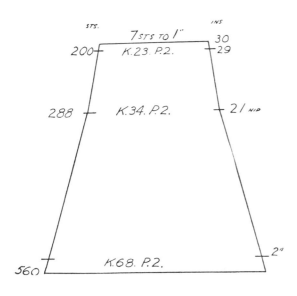

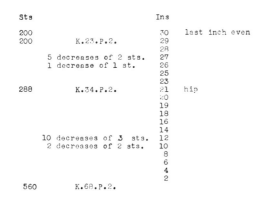

7 sts to the inch

Sts		Ins	
200		30	last inch even
200	K.23.P.2.	29	
		28	
	5 decreases of 2 sts.	27	
	1 decrease of 1 st.	26	
		25	
		23	
288	K.34.P.2.	21	hip
		20	
		19	
		18	
		16	
		14	
	10 decreases of 3 sts.	12	
	2 decreases of 2 sts.	10	
		8	
		6	
		4	
		2	
560	K.68.P.2.		

DIAGRAM 147

For gored skirts with different stitch gauges, use the same measurements as on page 241.

For an 8-gored skirt:

> Width at the bottom—80 inches
> Stitch gauge—7 stitches to the inch

1. Waist—29 inches x 7 stitches to the inch = 203 stitches, nearest number divisible by 8 is 200 stitches. 8 into 200 goes 25 times, i.e., K. 23, P. 2.

2. Hips—39 inches plus 2 inches = 41 inches x 7 stitches to the inch = 287 stitches, nearest number divisible by 8 is 288 stitches. 8 into 288 goes 36 times, i.e., K. 34, P. 2.

3. Width at the bottom—80 inches x 7 stitches to the inch = 560 stitches, divisible by 8 is 70 stitches, i.e., K. 68, P. 2.

4. Decreases

> Bottom to hips—34 stitches from 68 stitches leaves 34 stitches to be decreased in each gore; 3 stitches in each gore, 10 times, and 2 stitches in each gore, 2 times. See Diagram 147.
> Hips to waist—23 stitches from 34 stitches leaves 11 stitches to decrease in each gore, 1 stitch in each panel 11 times, first at one side, then the other.

For a 6-gored skirt with P. 1 between:

> Waist—29 inches
> Hips—39 inches plus 2 inches is 41 inches
> Length—31 inches (30 inches knitted length)
> Width at the bottom—76 inches
> Stitch gauge—7 stitches to the inch

1. Waist—29 inches x 7 stitches to the inch = 203 stitches, nearest number divisible by 6 is 204 stitches; 6 into 204 goes 34 times, i.e., K. 33, P. 1.

2. Hips—39 inches plus 2 inches = 41 inches x 7

stitches to the inch is 287 stitches, nearest number divisible by 6 is 288 stitches. 6 into 288 goes 48 times, i.e., K. 47, P. 1.

3. Width at the bottom—76 inches x 7 stitches to the inch = 532 stitches, nearest number divisible by 6 is 534 stitches, 89 times, i.e., K. 88, P. 1.

4. Decreases

Bottom to hips—47 stitches from 88 stitches leaves 41 stitches, i.e., 10 decreases of 4 stitches in each gore and 1 decrease of 1 stitch. First row of decreasing is as follows:—K. 1, K. 2 together, K. 26, K. 2 together, K. 26, K. 2 together, K. 26, K. 2 together, K. 1 (88 stitches), P. 1. See Diagram 148. Hips to waist—33 stitches from 47 stitches leaves 14 stitches; 2 stitches to decrease in each gore, 7 times.

CHAPTER 29

Page 173

For pleated skirts, use the same measurements as in Chapter 28.

Width at the bottom—76 inches, 2 inch pleats
Stitch gauge—7 stitches to the inch; therefore, 14 stitches in each pleat, 28 stitches in the knit and purl pleats together.

1. Width at the bottom—76 inches x 7 stitches to the inch = 532 stitches. 28 into 532 goes 19 times, making 38 ribs altogether.

2. Hips—39 inches plus 4 inches = 43 inches x 7 stitches to the inch is 301 stitches—use 304 stitches. 38 into 304 goes 8 times; therefore there are K. 8, P. 8 at the hips.

3. Waist—29 inches plus 2 inches = 31, x 7 stitches to the inch = 217 stitches. May be divisible by 19 or 38

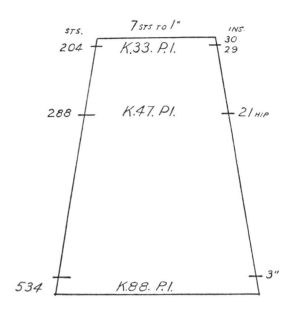

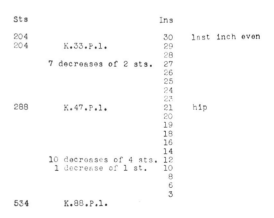

DIAGRAM 148

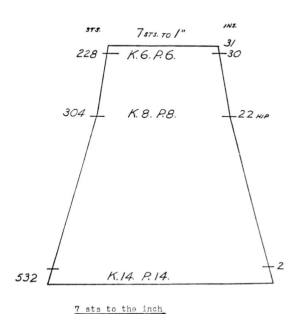

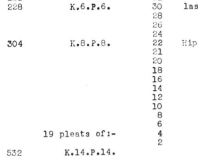

DIAGRAM 149

stitches; use 228 stitches. 38 into 228 goes 6 times, i.e., K. 6, P. 6 at the waist.

Suggest the higher number for pleated skirts.

4. Decreases

12 decreases first in the knit ribs, then in the purl to the hips.

Alternately decrease in the knit ribs, then the purl, every 2 inches to the waist. See Diagram 149.

CHAPTER 30

Page 177

For a 4-gored ribbon skirt or 4-gored machine-knit skirt:

Waist—29 inches
Hips—39 inches plus 4 inches = 43 inches
Width at the bottom—53 inches
Length—31 inches; $\frac{1}{2}$ inch crochet allowance in length, $30\frac{1}{2}$ inches
Half inch each side seam allowance for each panel or gore
Stitch gauge—5 stitches to the inch

1. Waist—29 inches divided by 4 is $7\frac{1}{4}$ inches plus 1 inch for seams = $8\frac{1}{4}$ inches x 5 stitches to the inch, or 42 stitches, even number.

2. Hips—39 inches plus 4 inches = 43 inches, divided by 4 is $10\frac{3}{4}$ inches, plus 1 inch for seams is $11\frac{3}{4}$ inches x 5 stitches to the inch, is 60 stitches, even number.

3. Width at the bottom—43 inches plus 10 inches = 53 inches, divided by 4 = $13\frac{1}{4}$, plus 1 inch equals $14\frac{1}{4}$ inches x 5 stitches to the inch or 72 stitches.

Diagram 150 is self-explanatory.

CHAPTER 33

Page 195

For a child's skirt of stockinette stitch:

      Waist—24 inches
      Length—19 inches
      Width at the bottom—48 inches
      Stitch gauge—6 stitches to the inch

  1. 48 inches x 6 stitches to the inch = 288 stitches; use 290 stitches.

  2. 24 inches x 6 stitches to the inch = 144 stitches; use 140 stitches.

  3. 290 stitches minus 140 stitches leaves 150 stitches to decrease, i.e., 7 decreases of 20 stitches, and 1 decrease of 10 stitches.

STITCHES		INCHES
		19 last in
140	K.6 (7.8)	18
160		17
		16
		14
		12
		10
		8
260	K.12 (13.14)	6
280	K.27 (28.29)	3
290 stitches		

For a pleated skirt:
Width at the bottom—52 inches and pleats 3 inches wide.
Stitch gauge—6 stitches to the inch

		INCHES
		19
144 stitches	K.8.P.8	18
		17

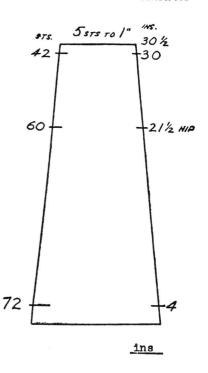

DIAGRAM 150

10 decreases in	16
each rib	14
	12
	10
	8
	6
	4
	2

324 stitches   K.18.P.18

1. Pleats 3 inches wide—3 x 6 stitches to the inch = 18 stitches. K. 18, P. 18 is 36 stitches.

2. Width at the bottom—52 inches x 6 stitches to the inch = 312 stitches; use 324 stitches to be divisible by 36 stitches. 36 into 324 goes 9, so 9 ribs of K. 18 and P. 18.

3. Width at the waist—24 inches x 6 stitches to the inch = 144 stitches. 18 into 144 goes 8 times, so there are K. 8, P. 8 at the waist.

Index